Doades, Joanne.
Parenting Jewish teens
: a guide for the perple
c2007.
33305211821628
la   02/05/07

Parenting *Jewish* Teens

A GUIDE FOR THE PERPLEXED

Joanne Doades

JEWISH LIGHTS Publishing

Woodstock, Vermont

www.jewishlights.com

Parenting Jewish Teens:
A Guide for the Perplexed

2007 First Printing
© 2007 by Joanne Doades

All rights reserved. No part of this book may be reproduced or transmitted in any form or by any means, electronic or mechanical, including photocopying, record-ing, or by any information storage and retrieval system, without permission in writing from the publisher.

For information regarding permission to reprint material from this book, please mail or fax your request in writing to Jewish Lights Publishing, Permissions Department, at the address / fax number listed below, or e-mail your request to permissions@jewishlights.com.

Grateful acknowledgment is extended to the following for permission to repro-duce their material in this book: Nine lines from p. 149 in *Exodus and Revolution* by Michael Walzer, Copyright 1985 by Basic Books. Reprinted with permission of Basic Books, a member of Perseus Books, L.L.C.; Central Conference of American Rabbis for permission to reprint the words of Thomas C. Short found in *Day to Day: Reflections on the Themes in the Torah from Literature, Philosophy, and Religious Thought,* edited by Chaim Stern, on page 281.

Library of Congress Cataloging-in-Publication Data
Doades, Joanne.
Parenting Jewish teens : a guide for the perplexed / Joanne Doades.
p. cm.
Includes bibliographical references.
ISBN-13: 978-1-58023-305-7 (pbk.)
ISBN-10: 1-58023-305-8
1. Child-rearing—Religious aspects—Judaism. 2. Jewish teenagers—United States—Religious life. 3. Jewish families—United States--Religious life. I. Title.
HQ769.3.D59 2007
296.7'4—dc22

2006030062

10 9 8 7 6 5 4 3 2 1

Cover design: Tim Holtz

Manufactured in the United States of America

Published by Jewish Lights Publishing
A Division of LongHill Partners, Inc.
Sunset Farm Offices, Route 4, P.O. Box 237
Woodstock, VT 05091
Tel: (802) 457-4000
Fax: (802) 457-4004
www.jewishlights.com

For Ron,
Jen, Rachel, and Aaron.
You are the blessings on my journey.

Contents

Acknowledgments

This book began as an offhand remark.

In what seems like a lifetime ago, literary agent Susan Ginsburg (known to me then as the mother of my son's best friend) was listening sympathetically as I bemoaned the challenges of parenting my Jewish teenagers. "I should write a book," I muttered, to which she replied, "I'd be interested in seeing it."

For the longest time, I couldn't bring myself to write it. My kids were quite far from perfect (body piercings, tattoos, beer cans in the closet, and worse), and my husband and I were sometimes out of control as we tried to navigate the turbulent waters of our children's teenage years. I often felt like I was drowning. Back then, a friend asked, "Well, if you can't write the book, who can?" I suggested a parent whose family always seemed so perfect. "Are you kidding?" my friend retorted. "Parenting Jewish teens is like walking through the valley of the shadow of death, and it looks like that's exactly what you've been doing!" Well, thanks, I guess.

Later, after I had passed through that valley, or at least the deepest parts of it, I developed a Parenting Jewish Teens workshop for parents and for Jewish communal professionals. Eventually, the workshop became the family education model in my master's thesis in religious education at Hebrew Union College–Jewish Institute of Religion. I told my thesis advisor, Dr. Eugene Borowitz, that I wanted to publish the thesis as a book. "It will take more work than this," he replied. And so it did.

I have been blessed along the way, from conversations to workshops to thesis to book, with many teachers, colleagues, and friends who have enabled me to take the vision of *Parenting Jewish Teens: A Guide for the Perplexed* to the reality it has become. Foremost among them is Dr. Eugene Borowitz, who has been teacher, rabbi, and dear friend to me. I am also grateful to Rabbi Dan Freelander and to Rabbi Jan Katzew, with whom I have the privilege of working and from whom I continually learn.

I am deeply indebted to the sensitive yet critical readers who reviewed *Parenting Jewish Teens* as it progressed and whose constructive feedback contributed significantly to the final product: Marilynn Jacobs, Rabbi Jan Katzew, Rabbi Len Levin, Sandy Merrill, Henry Resnick, Frances Schwartz, and editor Bryna Fischer.

My thanks to these professionals and friends who shared either their expertise or their personal stories, or both, to help me write Chapter 8 (Interdating and Intermarriage) and the appendix sections on special situations and situations that require intervention: Rabbi Richard Address, Rabbi Steve Bayar, Dr. Daniel Chesir-Teran and Ian Chesir-Teran, Rabbi Paula Mack Drill, Dr. Shana R. Ehrenberg, Rabbi Joan Glazer Farber, Margie Freeman and Len Levin, Deborah Gettes, Dr. Sol Gordon, Lori Jaffe, Jo Kay, Jackie and Michael Levinson, Rabbi Edythe Mencher, Rabbi Francine Roston, Dr. Evie Rotstein, and Ginny Twersky.

My agent, Susan Cohen of Writers House, provided guidance through challenging moments of the creative process, and I am grateful for her insights and constructive suggestions. In addition, I have received invaluable assistance from Hope Chernak, Amy Siglock, and Michael Goldberg.

I met Stuart M. Matlins, publisher and editor in chief of Jewish Lights, many years ago when Jewish Lights was just a dream and I was the harried mother of three little ones trying to find a place for myself and my family in the Jewish story. Who would have thought back then that his vision of Jewish Lights Publishing would some-day make my dream of writing a book about Jewish parenting come true? My deepest admiration for all that he has accomplished, and my thanks to his talented team of professionals, especially editorial vice president Emily Wichland and editor Lauren Seidman, for the work they have done in creating an enterprise with which I am so proud to be associated.

My husband and partner, Ronald, read every word of this book and has been my helpmate on this project every step of the way. I would never have believed that a person could be such a discerning yet gentle critic, but he is. Deepest thanks to him and to our beloved children, who have taught me that the real blessing of Jew-ish family life is learning how to change and grow—together.

Preface

In the year 1190, a book called The Guide for the Perplexed *was pub-lished. It was written by Moses ben Maimon, better known as Maimonides, the great Jewish medieval scholar, philosopher, physician, and codifier of Jew-ish law. His goal was to help scholars reconcile the truths of scripture with rational philosophy.*

One of my goals in writing Parenting Jewish Teens: A Guide for the Perplexed *is to help today's Jewish parents draw upon the teachings and the wisdom of our tradition in guiding their teens to adulthood.*

Rabbi Stuart Warner, a charismatic teacher whom my husband used to call "the Pied Piper of Jewish teens," was the principal of the community Jewish high school program our daughters attended for several years. I once broached the idea of a Parenting Jewish Teens workshop to him and he said words that struck me deeply. "You have no idea," he reported, "how many parents of Jewish teens just give up." I thought about that statement long and hard, especially since I myself had been seriously tempted to do just that. At a certain point, it can seem so much easier to shut down, to build a wall around your heart and insulate yourself from the onslaught of mystifying behaviors from your once-beloved-child-turned-incomprehensible-teenager. I've actually heard Jewish parents say everything from "Who cares what he does, it's his life," to "It doesn't matter what I say or do, she won't listen to me anyway," to "I don't have issues— my children have issues." (I'm still trying to figure that last one out.)

Giving up on our children, though, is not what parenting or Judaism is about. Judaism and parenting are about commitment, engagement, struggle, and growth, and ultimately renewal through change. Parenting Jewish teens today is about finding something to hang on to (Judaism works) as you try to hang on to your kids (don't give up, no matter what they look, smell, or act like). This book will tell you how the former can help accomplish the latter.

The idea for this book project was born from the difficulties of my own personal experience in parenting Jewish teens, and it was developed through my professional work. It was the topic of the thesis I submitted for my Master of Arts in Religious Education degree, awarded by Hebrew Union College–Jewish Institute of Religion in May 2001. In my work as a Jewish family educator and from my observations in presenting my Parenting Jewish Teens workshops at professional conferences, synagogues, and JCCs, I came to realize that Jewish parents across the spectrum often feel isolated and alone with their parenting Jewish teens issues and may not know how to access the power of our eternal tradition that purports to provide meaning and direction for a life well lived.

I arrived at this conclusion not from the viewpoint of a scholar, but from the perspective of the everyday Jew. My Jewish journey began in earnest when I was the parent of young children. I had grown up with virtually no Jewish education, in a sporadically affiliated but nonobservant home. Somewhere along the way I began to sense that there must be more to life's meaning than getting your toddler into a top New York City preschool. On my journey, I have studied and worshiped in countless Jewish settings, both religious and otherwise. The search for meaning is quite characteristic of our society, and I have realized that so many answers can be found within the Jewish tradition, as long as we are willing to reinterpret and apply its timeless messages to our own circumstance. *Parenting Jewish Teens* does just that.

Some Jewish parents seek answers to the questions that plague them by attending occasional presentations at their kids' school, where they will receive general parenting pointers. (It was in just such a place that I, for example, discovered that I wasn't the only parent in the world who believed that even a high school senior should have at least a nominal curfew, despite my daughter's impassioned protestations to the contrary.) Jewish parents can also read the many books available on the topic of parenting teens. A number of these deliver sound parenting advice, often administered with a dose of humor, presumably to ease the pain. *Yes, Your Teen Is Crazy!* is my current favorite title, though my guess is that if this book had been lying around when my kids were working their way through the teenage years, it would have been a bit like waving a red flag in the face of a raging bull. My sense is that even crazy people like teenagers can get touchy when they perceive—rightly or wrongly—that they are not being taken seriously.

But although resources such as local high school–based parenting lectures, books written by mental health professionals, and even private therapy sessions can provide tips, techniques, and important insights into the challenges of constructively parenting teenagers, for many Jewish parents, like me, this kind of help was not enough. There was a feeling that knowing the techniques and the strategies needed to survive the day-to-day struggles was helpful, but somehow lacking when the end of the day still found me physically, emotionally, and spiritually exhausted. What was it, then, that was missing?

We Jewish parents, and perhaps others as well, need a glimpse of the *meaning* that lies beyond the minute-by-minute, day-to-day encounters in the struggle of parenting emerging adults. In the everyday battles of life with our teens, we need the benefits and the comfort that the teachings and the wisdom that have guided and sustained the Jewish people through countless generations can provide. Because no one resource, including this book, can address every question and challenge parents of Jewish teens may face, we need to create our own communities of support, here and now, within synagogues, Jewish community centers, or other settings so we can learn from and help one another. Enabling us to do this is one of my hopes for *Parenting Jewish Teens: A Guide for the Perplexed.*

Special Situations

A story is told about a gentile (non-Jew) who asked the great first-century sage, Hillel, to teach him the entire Torah[1] while standing on one foot. Rather than react with indignation to such a blatantly mocking request, the wise Hillel stood on one foot and replied: "What is hateful to you, do not do to your neighbor. The rest is commentary. Go and study" (Babylonian Talmud,[2] *Shabbat* 31a). The man, as the legend is told, converted to Judaism and became a life-long student.

The first two appendices of this book touch upon topics that deserve deep, serious consideration, an entire Torah, if you will. But just as Hillel was not able to teach the entire Torah to a person while he stood on one foot, so it was not possible to include in *Parenting Jewish Teens: A Guide for the Perplexed* full consideration of what we should know about parenting at-risk teens or parenting special needs, adopted, or gay and lesbian teens, or teens whose parents are divorced. Instead, a brief introduction to each of these topics is presented, along with suggested resources for further study. The presentation of the material is based upon my research and upon my perspective as a Jewish educator. Parents should consult appropriate mental health professionals, where necessary.

I hope you will delve into these important subjects more deeply, whether or not you feel personally touched by them, because, as our tradition teaches us: "All Israel is responsible for one another" (BT, *Shavuot* 39a)—what affects one of us affects us all.

Introduction

1

This book is about a journey. You can take the journey alone, or we can take it together. Believe me, together is better.

From the time children enter adolescence and move through the teen years into young adulthood, most families enter a period that can be described as tumultuous, challenging, and chaotic. And sometimes, those are the good days. This is not just me talking: research has shown that marital satisfaction is at its lowest point during the years that teenagers are living in the home.[1]

Relationships with teenage children can be maddening and frustrating. They undergo the most peculiar transition from children we think we know into adolescents who become mysterious strangers we often wish we didn't. They spend much of their time in deep hiding, emerging unexpectedly to make demands, challenge our authority and sense of order in the world, and fill us with self-doubt and anxiety. They inspire us to feelings of embarrassment, rage, and hopelessness and drive us to behaviors we quickly regret. All of this happens as we, the parents, are trying to live a life, work outside or inside the home, and struggle with the impact our parents' parenting had on us. For the parents of Jewish teens, throw into this mix a desire to maintain a connection to the (choose as many as apply) traditions, practices, culture, identity, values, and observances of our Jewish tradition at just the same time that many of our teenagers are straining to go in the opposite direction. I think you can see the problem.

There are those who say that parenting teenagers has never been easy, that the struggle for independence is a timeless phenomenon. What changes in every generation, they say, are the artifacts—the symbols and the issues around which the struggle occurs. According to those who hold this position, there is, as the biblical writer known as Ecclesiastes might say, nothing new under the sun. Is it true that there has always been trouble between teens and their parents? Consider this:

> If a man has a wayward and defiant son, who does not heed his father or mother and does not obey them even after they discipline him, his father and mother shall take hold of him and bring him out to the elders of his town at the public place of his community. They shall say to the elders of his town, "This son of ours is disloyal and defiant; he does not heed us. He is a glutton and a drunkard." Thereupon the men of his town shall stone him to death. Thus you will sweep out evil from your midst: all Israel will hear and be afraid (Deut. 21:18–21).

This is a direct quote from the Torah, the first five books of the Hebrew Bible, which has essentially been the guidebook of the Jewish people for more than two thousand years. Whether you believe that the words it contains are the literal word of God or a compilation of texts that were put together in one final written form by about 450 BCE, we are still talking about the reference to a problem—a rebellious son—that has been going on for quite some time. (It should be noted that since we have received these texts from a tradition that was patriarchal, the stories, examples, and language are for the most part male, both in orientation and in focus. I can personally promise you, however, that teen rebellion can be observed in females as well.)

Getting back to the text, however, you might agree that the image is an interesting (appealing?) one. Here is what it says to me: if your kid is out of control, you can bring him (or her) before the community and the problem will be taken care of for you ... permanently. But before any of us rushes to such a solution, here are three points worth considering:

1. It never happened. No parents ever brought their rebellious son or daughter before the community to be executed. In all of Jewish history, our rabbis and scholars tell us, such an execution never occurred and never will (BT, *Sanhedrin* 71a). Still, the threat of the consequence had impact, or at least, that was the expectation.

2. Drinking and eating too much only tell part of the story. We really wouldn't kill someone for such behavior, since most of us engage in one or the other, or both, at least from time to time. The issue here, it seems to me, is that the behavior of the teen is so outrageous in terms of the values and standards of his or her home that the parents are distraught to the point where life is not worth living with that child—parent or teen has to go.

3. There was a community, a Jewish community, to which the parents of Jewish teens could turn with their problem. Then and now, parenting Jewish teens is a job that needs community support. For someone like me who felt so alone, even with a spouse, in the struggles of parenting Jewish teens, the thought of a community to turn to for comfort and guidance in the darkest moments holds great appeal. One of the reasons I am hoping that you and I can take the journey through this book—and through parenting Jewish teens—together is so that we can create such a community that will work for us, here, in our own time.

So it might seem, based on this Torah text, that there is, in fact, nothing new under the sun: parents in biblical days had, on occasion, some extreme trouble with teens, and so do we. In drawing upon my professional and personal experiences and observations, however, I do not believe that this is the case. Instead, I think that parenting Jewish teens today is different and infinitely more challenging than it ever was before. Why?

The World Has Changed

Parenting Jewish teens today is an experience without equal in all of our human and Jewish history. There are three interrelated conditions that make this so: consequences, culture, and community.

- Consequences. The rebellious son/daughter text gives us a window into a world in which there were serious consequences for behaviors that we might today term "way out of line." Until quite recently in fact, children, including teenagers, understood that boundaries existed that defined how far teenagers could go in bumping up against authority figures: parents, teachers, religious leaders, and law enforcement officials. Within the last generation and a half, however, there has been a radical change in attitudes of the young toward these institutional authorities, primarily as a result of the diminishment or the complete elimination of consequences for unacceptable behavior. In his delightful and insightful book, *Get Out of My Life, but first could you drive me and Cheryl to the mall?* Dr. Anthony Wolf describes the situation powerfully and succinctly: "This is the era of 'permissiveness.' As a result, the more fearsome weapons have been taken out of a parent's arsenal.... It's inevitable that without these harsher forms of enforcement, children's behavior has changed. This is just human nature. The new teenager does feel freer to do as he or she pleases, especially at home."[2]

  But please note the phrase "and all Israel will hear and be afraid" in our rebellious son/teen text. There are two Hebrew words that convey the meaning of fear. The root of one of them (*pey-chet-dalet*) literally means fear in the sense of physical safety. This is not the Hebrew term used in this text. Instead, the root of the word that is used, *yir'ah*, carries a meaning that is closer to respect and is often translated as "awe," a term that Rabbi Arthur Green explains this way: "Another understanding of *yir'ah* associates it with awe, a great sense of trembling before the greatness of God.... Awe causes us to distance ourselves from

God, not to become overly familiar, to take God's presence for granted. But this *yir'ah* also exists in balance with love."[3] This same sense of distance, awe, and respect traditionally characterized the relationship of children toward their parents, which carried with it an implicit sense or explicit understanding of consequences that set boundaries for behaviors. From what I can see, such a sense of boundaries is largely absent in most American Jewish families and throughout our society today.

• Culture. Today's popular culture generally depicts authority figures in the most unflattering light, either overtly or subtly. This is a marked change from the family programming of the past. For example, the brilliantly written and hilariously funny popular television program *The Simpsons* offers the following descriptions of some of its characters:[4]

> **Clancy Wiggum,** the chief of police: "The donut-scarfing, graft-accepting chief of the Springfield Police Department takes the law into his own hands, often making up his own laws right on the spot...."
>
> **Seymour Skinner,** the school principal: "When not conducting fire drills, augmenting the school lunches with shredded newspaper, polishing the statue of the school mascot, or calculating detention time for Bart, Skinner can be found at his desk, reliving ... the more horrific aspects of his experience as a Green Beret in 'Nam, an experience that serves him well in his current profession."
>
> **Mr. Burns,** the business executive who heads the utility company: "As the evil overlord of the Springfield Nuclear Power Plant, Burns tirelessly pursues even greater wealth and power through the exploitation of his hapless works and the destruction of the local environment."

I have always found *The Simpsons'* "leading men" characters objectionable because of their negative stereotyping of authority figures. Even worse, though, are many of the reality TV shows that glorify blatantly self-serving behavior. These shows portray as unscripted "real life" situations in which adults compete without scruples for rewards controlled by unfeeling power brokers. Emotionally manipulative to the extreme, some reality shows have become significant teachers of our children, sending negative messages to our teens about what it takes to "make it" in the adult world.

Do television models like these and other popular media create or simply reflect an erosion of decency and mutually respectful behavior in our culture today? We'll probably never know the answer to that question, but what we do know, what is distinctive and new today, is that the media, for the most part, *promote* this view. In other words, if we expect our teenagers to at least give us the semblance of respect, we are asking them to think counterculturally, to step outside their world, emotionally and intellectually. This may be more than they can readily do. As a result, conversations in our home, for example, often went something like this:

Me: "Don't you dare speak to me in that fresh tone of voice!"
She: "What are you *talking* about?? I'm not being fresh!"
Me: "You absolutely are! Don't talk to me like that!"
She: "I'm not talking fresh! I don't know what you want from me!"

Looking back on this period, I can picture two cartoons. In cartoon A, the mother is imagining herself as a teenager speaking to her own parents decades ago. She is fuming, she hates them, she thinks they are idiots, all of that, but she doesn't dare show it! In cartoon B, the daughter is imagining the way kids talk to parents in her cultural environment, and in comparison, she is an angel! For peace to prevail, both sides may have to give a little.

There are far more alarming issues about the peer pop culture of today's teens, however, than negative authority-figure role modeling and disrespectful speech. Most dangerous among these is the relationship between the virulently sexual and violent images so pervasive in the media and the behavior of our adolescents. The bottom line is that if you are trying to raise emotionally healthy, responsible, and respectful children and guide them safely through their teenage years, you may at times feel like David battling Goliath—and you are.

• Community. In his book *Bowling Alone,* Harvard professor Robert Putnam documents the trend toward an environment of increasing isolation and alienation from institutions in American culture. "The quantitative evidence is overwhelming, yet most Americans did not need to see charts and graphs to know that something bad has been happening in their communities and in their country. Americans have had a growing sense at some visceral level of disintegrating social bonds."[5] Jewish sociologists have noted similar trends within the American Jewish community: "The decline of communal obligations, the rise of sovereign individuals, is of course the modern story par excellence, one that has been told and retold by countless scholars of religion in the modern world," report Steven M. Cohen and Arnold M. Eisen in *The Jew Within: Self, Family, and Community in America.*[6]

The impact of this decline in communal connectedness on families has been nothing short of devastating. A report prepared by the Commission of Children at Risk reveals the following: "We are witnessing high and rising rates of depression, anxiety, attention deficit, conduct disorders, thoughts of suicide, and other serious mental, emotional, and behavioral problems among U.S. children and adolescents." In response to the question of what is causing this crisis, the report goes on to say, "In large measure, what's causing this crisis of American childhood is a lack of connectedness. We mean two kinds of connectedness—close connections to other people, and deep connections to moral and spiritual meaning."[7]

Throughout this book, we will explore the questions and the issues raised by these three characteristics—consequences, culture, and community—that shape the world in which our teenagers are living, and we will consider the response options that can help us maintain our sanity, our dignity, and our family relationships until the storm passes, or at least subsides, when our children reach young adulthood.

Hineini: Here I Am

"Where are you, Rachel? Are you hiding from Mommy?" My two-year-old daughter was crouching in the corner with her hands covering her eyes, giggling joyously in the belief that if she couldn't see me, I couldn't see her. Looking back, it seems as though that delightful stage of childhood lasted about one second. More recently, I remember other "where are you" questions left on cell phones: "Where are you? You didn't shovel the snow from the driveway and now I can't get the car out, so I can't get to work." "Where are you? It's three o'clock in the morning and we're worried sick about you." "Where are you? You swore you'd be home in time to come to synagogue with us this morning and we're sitting here waiting for you." "Where are you? The cleaning lady found beer cans in your closet and you'd better get your butt home right this minute!"

The Hebrew word *hineini* means "here I am." It appears several times in the Torah, when God, the heavenly parent, calls out to one of God's children. "Where are you?" God asks, and the response is, "Here I am."

Actually, the first time God calls out in this way, things don't work out so well. God, according to the text, is looking for Adam, who has disobeyed the one rule God established for him and his wife, Eve. Instead of responding, they hide (Gen. 3:8), and avoid facing the consequences of their actions. Reading the text as contemporary adults, however, we are led to wonder why God, who has the power to create the universe, can't figure out where Adam is. Why doesn't God just find Adam and confront him about his behavior? Why doesn't God simply say, "Look, Adam, I designed this magnificent world, I created you and gave you a beautiful wife, I made your life easy and stress-free, and all I asked was that you follow this one little rule. How could you have messed up so badly?" But that's not what happens. Instead, God goes searching for Adam, calling out to God's most precious work of creation, who is in hiding.

Later in our sacred text, however, God calls out to others, with better results. Abraham, the first Jew, responds, "*Hineini*—Here I am," when God wants to ask him to make the unbearably wrenching sacrifice of his only son, his beloved Isaac. Still later in the story of the Jewish people, Moses, the hidden Israelite child who grew to be a prince of Egypt, is now a fugitive tending his father-in-law's sheep in the desert. He hears God's call from the burning bush and Moses responds, "*Hineini*—Here I am," accepting the call to return to Egypt, at great risk to his own life, in order to free the Israelites from their generations of bondage there.

God, it seems, was not asking for a location statement in posing the question, "Where are you?" Instead, God was asking for something much more, something that we might translate into today's parlance as the much deeper question, "Are you there for me?"

"When the word *hineini* is uttered by biblical characters or by God, it generally connotes three main sentiments," according to Dr. Norman Cohen, provost of Hebrew Union College–Jewish Institute of Religion, in his book *Hineini in Our Lives: Learning How to Respond to Others through 14 Biblical Texts and Personal Stories* (Jewish Lights). "First is the ability to be present for and receptive to the other.... Second, the word indicates the readiness to act on behalf of the other.... Finally, *hineini* at times indicates the willingness to sacrifice for someone or something higher.... The nature of our relations is measured by our willingness to act for others or even to make sacrifices for others."[8]

Amid the annoying, terrifying, obnoxious, embarrassing, and incomprehensible behaviors that our Jewish teens often exhibit, could there be a small, frightened voice calling out to us, "Where are you, Mommy? Where are you, Daddy? Will you be with me as I leave that sweet childhood behind and enter the complex world of adulthood? Will you be with me as I grow to become someone we don't yet know?"

How will we respond, "*Hineini*"?

The Journey to *Hineini*

In this book, we will travel through the pain of separation (Chapter 2) as our children enter the world of teens today (Chapter 3). We will struggle with conflict (Chapter 4) and family relationships (Chapter 5), and we will explore the question of how to deal with differences in Jewish belief and observance within the same family (Chapter 6). We will examine how our own behaviors must change as our children grow older (Chapter 7), and we will take a look at interfaith issues as they affect our teen's lives today (Chapter 8). In Chapter 9, we will reflect back on our journey and discover an important insight into what it means to stay engaged with our children through the challenges and the blessings of their teenage years.

On this journey, we will do what Jewish parents have done throughout the generations: we will agonize, laugh, obsess, cry, and rejoice together. I hope that you will find comfort and guidance on these pages, and I hope you will feel the strength that being part of the Jewish community can provide. Most of all, I hope that you will be inspired to join or to begin a parenting Jewish teens group, such as the one described in Appendix C, so that you can continue the conversation—and the journey—together.

2

Separation

The process of separation begins at birth. The mother's body sustains, nurtures, nourishes, and protects the unborn child-to-be for about nine months, and then suddenly expels it into the world. The umbilical cord that had literally served as a lifeline is severed, and a struggle for survival begins.

Many years ago, my husband and I enrolled our daughter Rachel in the toddler program at Central Synagogue Nursery School in New York. At the orientation program before the beginning of school, the teacher for two-year-olds made a statement that struck me as odd. "Give your child the gift of separation," she said. She wasn't a mother and I, who was, had no idea what she was talking about. It has taken me almost twenty years to find out.

Between then and now, I have been on a crazy, impossible, and sacred journey as the mother of Jewish children, and I have learned important lessons about parenting today's Jewish teens from our timeless tradition. Separation is one of them.

Coming of Age

> *Baruch she'p'tarani me'onsho shel zeh.* Blessed is the One who has exempted me from the responsibility for this one.

Among Orthodox Jews, it is traditional for a father to utter this blessing at the bar mitzvah of his son. In doing so, the father publicly proclaims that he is no longer responsible for the errors or transgressions committed by the child who has come of age and who is now personally liable for his own mistakes. Most non-Orthodox Jews don't recite this blessing these days; instead, they say the *Shecheyanu* blessing to thank God for enabling them to reach this joyous occasion.

So why include the *baruch she'p'tarani* blessing in a book about today's Jewish teens?

Because it marks, in a way that no other ritual associated with this event does, a Jewish child's coming of age. According to Jewish law, a child who reaches the age of thirteen accepts responsibility for obeying the commandments. And though this blessing may only be symbolic for most of us, it is interesting to note that for many generations, Jewish fathers have publicly proclaimed a change in family status on the occasion of their sons' thirteenth birthday, the age we modern Jews note as the beginning of the teenage years.

Why is thirteen the bar or bat mitzvah age? Is it because, as the legend goes, our patriarch Abraham shattered his father's idols at age thirteen, or because it was understood by our rabbis of long ago to be a time of significant change and the beginning of adulthood? We don't really know the answer to this question, but we do know that at this most self-conscious time of life we ask our somewhat awkward children to stand before a huge audience and to demonstrate a leadership and mastery of skills that would be daunting, if not impossible, for most adults. It is, as our rabbi of many years Jehiel Orenstein once observed, crazy. "But what's crazier is," he exclaimed, "they do it!"

The moment of bar and bat mitzvah generally represents a new beginning in some respects, and a bittersweet ending in others. For the child, it can mean the exhilarating entry into the life of a teenager, a giant step toward adulthood and ultimate independence. For the parent, however, it is often a signal that the all-powerful role of "mommy" or "daddy" to a vulnerable and adoring child is drawing to a close.

The message of the *baruch she'p'tarani* blessing, whether we say it for our own children or not, calls to our attention the deeper significance of the bar or bat mitzvah event—the separation between childhood and the teenager years.

Leaving Home—Three Ways to Go

Many of the changes that accompany the life-cycle event of bar and bat mitzvah are physical in nature. It is the time of puberty. The thirteen-year-old may already be well along in this process, or soon will be. For girls, changes directly related to the ability to bear children unfold: the breasts develop and menstruation begins. Boys find themselves with new and deeper voices and the very beginnings of facial hair. Both sexes will soon be subject to raging hormones that are the source of powerful and sometimes frightening feelings, and many adolescents will be faced with the dreaded pimples that will become the focus of much consternation and preoccupation. But the physical changes that begin to occur or accelerate at this age are only a part of the story; the bigger tale is the drama that will play out in every family as the child, once held so closely and so lovingly, struggles to break free of that embrace.

The Book of Genesis, the first book of the Torah, has been providing the Jewish people with fascinating models of family dynamics and relationships, both good and bad, for more than two thousand years. Though the stories are set in biblical times, their messages are amazingly timeless, as the voices of those who came before speak to us in a language that is both enduring and comforting, and can offer direction and guidance to help us find our way. The following three stories about leaving home give us such a message.

Abraham

In the Torah portion *lech l'kcha* ("Go forth"), God speaks directly to Abram, who will later be renamed Abraham:

> The Lord said to Abram, "Go forth from your native land and from your father's house to the land that I will show you. I will

make of you a great nation and I will bless you." … Abram
went forth as the Lord had commanded him (Gen. 12:1–4).

One of the questions we might ask of this text is this: If Abram is to
leave his native land, isn't he also, by definition, leaving his father's
house? Why the apparent redundancy?

During the hippie drug culture of the1960s, it was considered
really cool to go to California to "get your head together," whatever
that meant. No one, of course, actually got their head together by
just going to California, or anywhere else for that matter. Changes
in the external environment, however pleasant, don't solve one's
problems or change one's life. Perhaps this was God's message to
Abram: You must leave the place in which you live (your native
land) *and the influence and teachings of your past* (your father's house)
to become the leader of a great, new nation, one that I will bless
and that will be a blessing.

Jacob

Abraham's son Isaac married Rebekah, and she gave birth to twin
sons. Esau was an outdoorsy hunter kind of guy, and his dad favored
him. Rebekah, on the other hand, preferred Jacob, who enjoyed
staying close to home, cooking with his mother, and studying.
When Isaac was old, almost blind, and ailing, Rebekah devised a
scheme to deceive her husband so that he would give Jacob both
the birthright and the blessing rightfully due Esau, their firstborn
son. In one of the most poignant and painful scenes in the Torah,
Esau weeps upon learning of this spectacular deception and asks,
"Have you but one blessing, Father? Bless me too, Father!" (Gen.
27:38). Isaac complies, but the blessing is a lesser one and the
birthright has already been given to Jacob. Here is what followed:

> Esau harbored a grudge against Jacob because of the blessing
> which his father had given him and Esau said to himself, "Let
> but the mourning period of my father come, and I will kill my
> brother Jacob." When the words of her older son, Esau, were

reported to Rebekah, she sent for her younger son Jacob and said to him, "Your brother is consoling himself by planning to kill you. Now, my son, listen to me. Flee at once ..." (Gen. 27:41–43).

Escaping before Esau could get his hands on him, Jacob began a journey that would have profound implications for the Jewish people. The Torah does not reveal Jacob's age at the time of his flight from his parents' home, though it seems likely that he was a teenager. Caught between his mother's preference for him and his father's preference for his brother, Esau, Jacob was forced to make a life-and-death decision in the most literal sense—leaving his family and the only world he had ever known meant survival.

Joseph

Jacob eventually had twelve sons and one daughter. His son Joseph was the older of the two sons born to Jacob's beloved wife, Rachel. Jacob unabashedly favored him over his eleven other sons. This family's stories are many, but probably the most famous one is about the beautiful coat of many colors that Jacob gave to Joseph (popularized more than three thousand years later in the Broadway show *Joseph and the Amazing Technicolor Dreamcoat*). Not surprisingly, their father's favoritism toward Joseph infuriated the other brothers: "And when his brothers saw that their father loved him more than any of his brothers, they hated him so that they could not speak a friendly word to him" (Gen. 37:4). The result was that, at their earliest opportunity, the brothers threw Joseph into a pit and then solved their problem of what to do with him by selling him to passing traders who brought Joseph to Egypt and sold him there.

These stories from our Bible, our people's sacred text, describe three important journeys that began very differently. Abraham left home voluntarily, at God's request, with the promise of great reward. Jacob also left home "voluntarily," though truth be told he had little choice—to stay literally meant to die. And Joseph had no choice whatsoever. His brothers got rid of him, sending him into what they thought would be permanent exile. So what is the connection between the stories of Abraham, Jacob, and Joseph, and what do they have to teach us about parenting Jewish teens today?

The answer lies in what happened to Abraham, Jacob, and Joseph *after* they left home. What was the *result* of their leaving? They each amassed great wealth and achieved enormous status, both in their own day and in the meta-story of our people. Abraham and Jacob are remembered as patriarchs and Joseph as a leader whose later-in-life reconciliation with his brothers provides a stirring model of forgiveness and repentance to this day. If there is a message behind these texts, it seems to be that in order to be truly successful, you need to leave your parents' home.

The leaving home, of course, is more than a physical event. It symbolizes a state of mind and the development of one's own identity. In order to grow to one's fullest potential, the text seems to be telling us, you must "leave your father's house" behind.

For the child, this is exhilarating business. The teenage years, though generally lived mostly at home in our culture, very much mark the beginning of a journey of separation and distancing from parental values, attitudes, and controls. It's a time of great experimentation, of trying on new beliefs, new styles, and new personas to learn what works, what connects, what to adapt, and what to discard. For the parents, though, this is a time of letting go, as children grow into forms, voices, and behaviors we often don't recognize—or like. So what about us, those who are left behind when our children embark on their journeys? What does this feel like, and what does it mean?

My husband and I have three children. I wanted a fourth. My husband would gladly have stopped at one. ("What do we need more for? She's perfect!") He ultimately articulated a statement that I believed had some merit: "You'll always want just one more," he pointed out.

Many Orthodox families don't have this problem. The mother continues having babies in keeping with what is considered the first of 613 biblical commandments—"be fruitful and multiply"—throughout her childbearing years. It is often the case that when the mother stops having children, the oldest offspring have married and started having babies themselves. There are always babies. Not so for most of us. The babies grow, slowly at first, then shockingly quickly, and soon they are teenagers, positioning themselves to move on and leave us behind. For parents like me, this is hard stuff. I was scared. I resisted. I fought. I made things far more difficult than they had to be. I resented her for wanting to be Jen instead of Jenny (hmm, didn't Abraham, Sarah, and Jacob have transformative name changes, too?). What in the world was going on?

I wanted that little girl back, the one who would throw herself into my lap, shrieking: "Read me! Read me!" I wanted that little boy back, the one who would knock over his building-block constructions and race to the front door at the sound of my key in the lock. Now her door was shut so tight I doubted she would ever come out, and the music was blasting so loud in his room that I doubted he would have heard twenty people storming the house. The separation process that is (mostly) so exciting for our children can be deeply painful for us, a topic we will explore further in Chapter 7. But as we let our children go, little by little and piece by piece, what will we give them to take on their journeys? What teachings from our tradition can we share with them to help them navigate through the complicated and often dangerous landscape that has become the territory of the American teenage years?

The Sacred and the Profane

A significant and value-laden aspect of separation can be found in the Havdalah ceremony that marks the end of the weekly Sabbath on Saturday evening. Separation is explained as a distinction between what is sacred (the Sabbath) and what is "profane" or ordinary (the days of the workweek). A deeper message Jews can derive from this practice is that there is a distinction to be made between what is a special (we could say "holy") and what is a profane, ordinary, part of our everyday lives. The final blessing thanks God, the One who separates the holy from the profane/ordinary. From the root letters for the key word *holy (kadosh)* come a number of words that carry this special meaning, including the Hebrew word for marriage, *kiddushin.* For Jews, the idea of setting things apart in a consecrated way is fundamental. It teaches us to think about what we are doing and about the choices we are making. For true believers like me, God's presence is reflected in the choices we make, as we, in effect, ask ourselves the question: how does what I am doing reflect my values and my highest aspirations for myself? How does any given choice I make help make the world a better (holier) place?

During the year that our family contained three teenage children, I at some point realized that I wasn't going to have the control that I wanted over everything my children saw and heard in the world. Though my husband and I had done a pretty good job, we thought, of limiting TV viewing hours and objectionable shows and prohibiting TVs and computers in their bedrooms, it was impossible to keep the outside world outside. We were horrified, of course, at what we were seeing and hearing when we dared to look and listen: the shocking eroticism of television shows and commercials; the representation of sexual interactions as a casual, lighthearted activity; the depiction of women as, let's not mince words, complete sex objects whose sole purpose is to attract, arouse, and satisfy a man's sexual "power" (and, yes, any man will do)—to name a few. (As a child of the women's movement, I'm still dumbfounded by all this. What happened?!)

If you think I am overstating or overreacting to this situation, I recommend that you somehow find out what your teenager is really listening to and watching, and find a way to listen and watch, too. In our case, there were times when I would walk into our family room while one of our teenage children was in front of the TV. On several occasions, I was told that what he or she was watching "wasn't appropriate" for me (this was code for "too sexy," "containing profanity," "morally objectionable"), with the suggestion that I wouldn't be comfortable remaining. I was so shocked the first few times it

happened that, I'm embarrassed to admit, I just said something profound, like, "Oh," and left the room. After I had regrouped, however,
I taught myself to say, "If this program is not appropriate for me, it's
certainly not appropriate in our home, so it has to go because I'm
not leaving." Not quite brilliant, but it worked.

Still, it wasn't and isn't possible to prevent our children from
experiencing the media that surround them, no matter how much
we would like to. For example, my sister returned to Judaism in a
big way and lives in a Hasidic[1] community in Brooklyn, New York,
the American center of Lubavitch Judaism. In such communities,
there is a strong taboo against home TVs for the same reasons I
would have liked to keep much of what is presented on television
out of my home, too. That community is not 100 percent successful,
and I was far less so. And television is just part of the problem—there
is the Internet, music, billboards, and other advertising, all of which
present mindless, irrelevant sexual attraction and interaction as important to status and self-esteem, the absolute opposite of the longer-term
consequences of early sexual activity. Why? Because it sells products by
creating a culture of satisfaction through acquisition.

As soon as I reluctantly recognized the limited, if not nonexistent, control I personally had over my children's viewing and listening choices, I realized that an important shift was taking place in our
relationship. Since I could no longer ensure that things would happen the way I thought they should, I had to find a way to give my
children the tools they needed to evaluate their own choices.

I gathered them together in one of those little family meetings
that seemed to be so successful in other homes, but which were
absolutely awful in ours. I pushed all the thoughts about the daily,
here-and-now struggles of our lives out of my mind and I spoke to
them from my heart of hearts. I told them that I knew the world
outside our home could be a wonderful place, and a dangerous one.
I told them that they would no doubt experience much beauty in
their lives, and much ugliness as well. I told them that as their mom,
I could no longer protect them from all evil and harm, and that they
would no doubt make some choices that would cause them great

suffering. Finally, I told them that, as the Torah teaches us (a great rolling of three sets of eyes here), the world we live in is not the Garden of Eden—good and evil are equal possibilities. I reminded them that we learn as Jews that we have the power to choose, and that each decision we make is our personal responsibility. In making those choices, I asked them to think about all that they had learned from our home and from their Jewish education and to try to identify and separate the sacred from the profane when making decisions about what they will do and what they won't. "This is the power that God gives each one of us," I said. "I pray that you will use that power well."

The eyes had stopped rolling. After a moment or two, one of them said, "Can we go now?" And off they went.

3

Our Teenagers: American and Jewish

When I was growing up, American Jews still had a foothold (well, maybe a toehold) in the Old World. My parents surely loved America, especially my father, who as a little boy had learned as much about being Jewish from the pogroms of his native Russia as he had from the *heder,* the Jewish school, that taught him the prayers and the rituals of his forefathers' tradition. Parents like my dad never missed an opportunity to let the children of my generation know how lucky we were to have been born here, and I never for a minute doubted him on this.

But when he and his six older siblings would get together, they would talk for hours, sharing their memories with each other in a mixture of heavily accented English and occasional Yiddish (especially for the spicier parts of the stories we kids weren't supposed to understand). In those exchanges, I glimpsed a world so different from anything I could imagine in my own. For all its very real threats and dangers, and for all its deprivation and poverty, that Old World experience of my father and his siblings seemed to have had a quality of warmth, community, and connectedness that most of us have not been able to replicate here in America, even to this day. I think the enduring popularity of the play, the movie, and the music of *Fiddler on the Roof* is an expression of the longing that many American Jews feel, either consciously or unconsciously, for a life that seemed so well defined by shared values, practices, and communal relationships.

Jews in America

Jews left those foreign shores and came to America for the very same reasons that others did. We, and they, fled intolerance and oppression and we, and they, sought economic and social opportunity. The New World welcomed those who were willing to take the risks associated with such a displacement, and it richly rewarded those who succeeded here. That environment encouraged a strong feeling of individualism that led to and was supported by the political system of democracy, which, in turn, fostered the belief in individual rights that is so characteristic of the American mind-set today.

For Jews, one of the consequences, or the price, of success in America has been assimilation as a way of fitting in to the larger culture. In his seminal work, *American Judaism: A History,* Professor Jonathan D. Sarna describes the situation, and the conflict, this way: "A ... challenge confronting American Judaism concerns contemporary culture. Sexual freedom, gender equality, personal autonomy, gay and lesbian rights, openness to intermarriage, and a host of other liberal twenty-first-century American values raise anew one of modern Judaism's perennial questions: accommodate to contemporary culture or resist it?"[1]

Depending upon where you sit on the spectrum from secular to extremely observant, you and your Jewish family will confront a variety of issues and questions that will affect your family dynamics and determine your attitude about acceptable behaviors. For the parents of Jewish teens, these interactions can sometimes be wrenching, as teenage rebellion is often played out against Jewish values. This topic is addressed in Chapter 6 (Jewish Observance: Yours, Mine, and Ours), but for our present purposes, suffice it to say that navigating the teenage years with the hope that your children's behavior will reflect the positive Jewish values you may have knowingly or unconsciously taught until this point can be difficult at best, and impossible at worst. Let's take a look.

The American Teen Landscape

The second half of the twentieth century saw a dramatic change in the role of the teenager in American life. No longer were teenagers viewed as adults in training, as they had previously been. Instead, they emerged as a separate, distinct group with a mystique all their own. By the early 1960s, teens were seen, at their worst, as rebellious, unpredictable, and defiant bordering on the dangerous. At their best, they were seen as daring and free-spirited in a way that inspired a touch of wistful longing in more mature adults who had exchanged their youthful playfulness for the responsibilities of family life.

Until recently, the changes from childhood to adolescence were believed to be most influenced by the hormonal development that biologically prepared humans of both sexes for their reproductive roles. Raging hormones were thought to be responsible for teen moodiness, unpredictability, and risk-taking behavior. More recently, studies of brain development and brain activity now possible through advances in technology provide a new world of information about what is—and isn't—going on inside the teen mind. Particularly interesting, at least for parents like me, are revelations about the difficulty teens naturally have in doing such things as correctly reading and interpreting social signals, such as facial expressions; making discerning judgments; and organizing and prioritizing several tasks successfully, according to a number of recent studies, including a PBS *Frontline* report, "Adolescent Brains Are Works in Progress."[2] Although these limitations may not have serious consequences in and of themselves, what is alarming is the unprecedented access that our children have to risky behaviors at this immature stage of their development.

While many teenagers make it through this transition relatively smoothly, an increasingly large number are hitting significant bumps along the way. If you haven't been keeping up with the current literature about the world of today's teens, brace yourself. The picture is not a pretty one. On the whole, teenagers are engaging in risky behaviors in far greater numbers than responsible, caring parents would care to know. In fact, many of us don't know. "Once a teen has decided what she's going to do, she may feel there's no point in upsetting her parents by exposing them to information they couldn't handle," asserts Dr. Linda Sonna in *The Everything Parenting a Teenager Book: A Survival Guide for Parents!* "Most modern teens are quite protective of their parents, who they see as chronically stressed and easily overwhelmed."[3] Parental awareness or the lack of it notwithstanding, our children are coming of age in an era characterized by rising rates of sexually transmitted diseases, binge drinking, drug addiction, and self-destructive behaviors. Here are some indicators to consider:

- According to a study published in the April 2005 issue of *Pediatrics* magazine, one in five ninth-graders reported having oral sex and one-third planned to try it within the next six months.[4]

- By age thirteen, the average teen has witnessed 100,000 incidents of television violence and watched unwed couples engage in sexual activity on dramas at the rate of twice per hour.[5]

- A 2004 Rand Corporation study found that there is a direct relationship between TV watching and early sexual initiation among teens. "Youths who viewed the greatest amounts of sexual content," the report noted, "were two times more likely than those who viewed the smallest amount to initiate sexual intercourse during the following year or to progress to more-advanced levels of other sexual activity."[6]

- Teenage alcohol misuse, a widely increasing phenomenon, is particularly worrisome because of its association with accidents, suicide, violent behavior, high-risk sex, and emotional problems, according to a Rand Corporation study.[7]

- More than 5 million high school students admit to binge drinking at least once a month, according to a study by Columbia University. The same study points out that underage drinking is an epidemic in the United States and now germinates in elementary and middle school.[8]

- Twenty percent of eighth-graders have been drunk at least once.[9]

I think that the compelling, highly sexualized images from the media that appeal to teens' need to be attractive, popular, and cool are much to blame for a good part of this problem. This is an extremely profitable marketing strategy, however, with teens representing an $89 billion market, in addition to the estimated $200 billion that their parents spend on them.[10] Teens are big, big business, and those who wish to sell products to them do not seem inclined to exercise appropriate restraint in fashioning their messages. "Adolescents and teenagers who regularly watch prime-time television are offered a steady mix of marital infidelity, casual sex, the objectification of women, and exploitative relationships," reports researcher Barrie Gunther in "Does Media Sex Influence Young People?"[11]

Compounding the sexualized marketing blitz aimed at today's teenagers is the fact that their parents are often not home during the many hours of free teen time, so teens are often placed in the position of making viewing, listening, and activity choices without guidance from a responsible parent. *Newsweek* magazine reports: "As a group, they lead lives that are more 'adult-free' than those of previous generations.... When today's teens are not with their friends, many live in a private, adult-free world of the Web and videogames."[12] A 1999 Kaiser Family Foundation report, *Kids and the Media,* observed that "children's bedrooms are rapidly becoming 'media central,' offering most kids the chance to consume many kinds of media in the privacy of their own rooms." According to Dr. Ron Taffel:

> For as long and as late as they like, they listen to music, watch programs, or visit Internet sites that their parents know little or nothing about. This leaves them in their own universe, where loyalty is less to their own families than to the kid culture and the closed society of their peers.[13]

It seems that the schools in which our teenagers spend so much of their time are not positioned to be of much help. A 2002 survey of guidance counselors found that none reported spending time directing students' moral growth or serving as their mentors or friends. Instead, they spent their time arranging class schedules, dealing with college applications, and addressing such administrative matters as attendance and school discipline.[14]

Where Are Jewish Kids in This Picture?

Given this landscape, who are today's American Jewish teens and how do Jewish teens compare with their counterparts in the general population? What makes a Jewish teen "Jewish"?

As a Jewish mother and educator, I believed for many years that "Jewishness" provided a kind of mysterious inoculation against the dangers of the secular teen culture. I thought that raising kids in Judaism would somehow give them something extra, like the additional *nefesh* (soul) that is said to remain with us as we enter the new week after the conclusion of Shabbat. I thought that by creating a Jewish home for my children, and by helping other parents do the same, we could block out or at least minimize the excesses of the teen pop culture and move our children safely through the environment described by the preceding statistics.

My children, of course, thought this was a ridiculous fantasy, and they didn't mind telling me so. The older two didn't waste much of their time trying to convince me, but the youngest did. Maybe it was because he was the only one of the three who attended a Jewish day school and he didn't want all the burdens of my expectations placed on his young shoulders (too bad, he got them anyway). Maybe it was because he was frustrated by my short-sighted and unfair double standard that lumped non-Jewish teens into a single category, which implicitly insulted such beautiful kids as his own first cousins on his father's side (whoops, right about that). Or maybe it was because he wanted a mom who lived in the real world and could be available to talk about it in a real way (I'm working on it).

Whatever the case, with great *derech eretz* (gentleness, sensitivity) tinged with occasional impatience, my son, Aaron, repeatedly tried to convince me that Jewish teens are no different than the teen population in general. Did I believe him? Not for a minute. Is he right? Here is the answer from a study of Reform, Conservative, and Reconstructionist Jewish teens conducted by the Cohen Center for Modern Jewish Studies at Brandeis University: "Rates of sexual activity and drug use (mainly alcohol and marijuana) were similar to those for comparable national samples of teenagers. Except for the youngest group, Jewish commitments appeared to have little influence on sexual activity and drug use."[15]

I think it's fair to say that the organized Jewish community (a term that is, in many respects, an oxymoron) has, in most cases, been stonewalling on the issue of Jewish teens and risky behaviors right into the present.[16] The reasons are many, and not the subject of our focus here, but a sampling of the stories that are breaking through the kosher wall of silence gives us a glimpse:

- An anonymous chat list, thelockers.net, was established for Orthodox teens in the New York tristate area to provide an opportunity for Orthodox youth who are struggling with drug and alcohol use to receive help and advice. The founder, Rabbi Yehoshua "Shu" Eliovson, states: "The goal is to coax the community forward to face the truth in a way that is good for kids and will not have the community react in a way that is very destructive for the kids."[17]

- According to Rabbi Joel Dinnerstein, former director of the Yatzkan Center in New York City, the first kosher in-patient rehabilitation center for young people with addictions, 60 percent of Jewish teens at any kind of school have tried some illegal or controlled substance.[18]

- At a party in affluent Livingston, New Jersey, in the fall of 2004, forty-two teens, most of whom attended Orthodox yeshivas and area Jewish days schools, were arrested and charged with possession of marijuana and possession or consumption of an alcoholic beverage by a minor.[19]

- The Winter 2003–2004 issue of *Lilith* magazine carried a feature story called "It's Not Sex," about young Jewish teenage girls who perform oral sex on boys in such settings as school and the back of the bus en route to bar and bat mitzvah parties.[20]

What's a (Jewish) Parent to Do?

On a personal level, I guess my ideas about what Jewish behaviors are and what they are not haven't exactly reflected the realities of life in the teenage world today. I was shocked, for example, when one of my children announced that the belly ring on her body was obtained during a Jewish community–sponsored teen trip to Israel. (Had I somehow given her the impression that I'd be less upset because its place of origin made it somehow "Jewish"?) Judaism prohibits self-mutilation of the body, which includes tattooing and body piercing, as a negation of the holiness of the body *(kedushat ha-guf),* though my reaction was more personal than religious: why would my beautiful child, I wondered, want to have someone cut her flesh?

Be that as it may, I have, based on my personal and professional experience, developed a few lessons learned—best practices, if you will—that I'd like to share with you if you are parenting Jewish teens or in any way invested in assisting people who are. These may not inoculate teenagers against every danger out there, but they will help guide you through so that you can: (a) know that you did your job and (b) find a place to meet when they emerge on the other side as (mostly) intact twenty-somethings:

1. Stay as close as you can, even when they hate you. I know "hate" is a strong word and some people really object to it, but it catches the flavor of feelings that can find their way into a household in which teenagers are present. Chapter 4 will address the topic of dealing with conflict and you'll hopefully find more specific helpful tips there; for now, suffice it to say that you must stay involved with your teen and her life, no matter what the circumstances of any miserable given moment may be.

2. Don't waste time preaching sermons in a foreign language; make your message realistic enough to be comprehensible, and focus on their health and safety. Telling today's teens to abstain completely from anything except the most obviously dangerous behaviors will have no real effect. Instead, engage in conversations about the issues that concern you the most, such as sex that is early or unprotected or both, and drinking and drugs. Study after study has shown that most kids will experiment with risky behaviors, no matter what we tell them. The message from expert research seems to be this: get the conversation going, keep it going, and make it real. Focus on your love for them and your concerns about their health and safety, now and over the long term. Send them the message that you are watching over them in a way that is both the same and different as when they were little. They may push back on this, but ask yourself: wouldn't you like to know that there was someone watching over *you,* ready to catch *you* if you were about to fall?

3. Insist on maintaining your parental role of supervision, even though it must shift a little as we enable our children to move toward independence (the subject of Chapter 7). Don't let your teen go to unsupervised parties, and don't allow one in your home. Do not be intimidated by your teen's objection to your checking up on this. This is your job as a parent, and this aspect of your role is more important now than it ever was before. However, this is not a fail-safe. I have learned that although some parents are home for their kids' parties, they may be sequestered away to give the kids "privacy." You won't always know about this until after the fact, if even then. Do the best you can to ensure that there will at least be a parental *presence* connected to the party.

4. Watch what they watch and listen to what they listen to. Ask real questions, not didactic or judgmental ones, to engage them in conversation and help them make more discerning judgments about pop culture. When music videos were becoming the rage,

for example, I would sometimes sit and watch with my daughters and express my surprise at the glorified depiction of females as erotic sex objects. Whatever happened, I would wonder out loud, to the quite opposite goals of the women's movement? (I'm still wondering.)

5. Find or begin a parenting Jewish teen group. How to do this is included in Appendix C, but suffice it to say that the job of parenting Jewish teens is too tough to do alone, or even with a partner. It takes a Jewish community to raise Jewish children, always has, always will. Most of us needed help when our children were little, and we surely need it when they are teenagers. Judaism can teach us much about this subject (that's what this book is about) and about being part of a caring community that shares your spiritual and emotional values. This is important and necessary in order to sustain and renew you as you work to sustain and renew your teenage child.

In reflecting on all this, I'm led to wonder: could it be that there is more to this experience of parenting Jewish teens than just surviving it? Could it be that God is somehow working in this process and that we need to pay more attention to what is actually going on here? Might there be a *reason* for our suffering through our children's teenage years, a rationale to engage, confront, and "be there" in a way that at first glance escapes our comprehension?

Let's see whether there is a message we can discern in the confusing, challenging, and humbling experience of parenting Jewish teens.

4

Dealing with Conflict

Two weeks before Rachel's bat mitzvah, the long-overdue final payment to the caterer was firmly affixed to our refrigerator door. "It stays there," I announced sanctimoniously, "until the rabbi and the cantor tell me that there *will* be a bat mitzvah." Rachel hadn't yet begun writing her bat mitzvah speech, which in our congregation was expected to be a fairly significant teaching.

We were having a hard time.

Maybe part of the problem was that neither my husband nor I had ourselves experienced the bar/bat mitzvah preparation process at age thirteen, and we didn't know how excruciatingly difficult it could be. Or maybe I expected Rachel to lock herself in her room and just do it, whatever "it" was, like her older sister had. Or maybe I didn't realize how hard it must have been for a barely thirteen-year-old girl to compose a meaningful speech for an audience of hundreds about bodily emissions and skin diseases, the subject of her Torah portion. Or maybe I was just plain stupid.

Our rabbi, on the other hand, was wise. He looked at our struggling daughter with tenderness and calmly asked, "Rachel, is there anything in this Torah portion that speaks to you, that has meaning for you, that causes you to react in any way at all?"

"Yes," she retorted, "in the Torah people were put outside the camp because they had skin diseases or something wrong with them. That's how I feel when we say the *Amidah*[1] and we only say the names of the patriarchs, like the women weren't our ancestors, too! I feel excluded, like I don't belong."

"Fine," the rabbi calmly responded as I sat in shocked disbelief, "speak about that."

The rest, as they say, is history. Here is how it was reported in the *New Jersey Jewish News.*

> Congregation Beth El in South Orange was pushed into the liturgy debate when congregant Rachel Doades was preparing for her bat mitzvah ceremony.... Rachel said the unfair treatment of lepers was like the unfair treatment of women in Judaism, especially the lack of inclusion of the matriarchs along with the patriarchs in the *Amidah.* [Rabbi] Orenstein told her to make that the subject of her *d'var Torah.*[2]

So while I was busy threatening the kid with the public humiliation of no bat mitzvah if her speech wasn't ready, the rabbi had the wisdom to push all the normal expectations aside and reach into my daughter's soul. The result was the beginning of a fairly peaceful liturgical revolution in our synagogue, for which Rachel's bat mitzvah speech deserves much credit.

Obviously, the rabbi had learned some lessons about conflict resolution that I had not.

Somewhere near the beginning of the Parenting Jewish Teens workshop that I lead, I ask the parents to identify the issues that really drive them crazy about their kids. In less than a minute, we usually get a list that looks something like this:

- Messy room
- Fresh talk
- Laziness (general)
- Laziness (about schoolwork)
- Money
- Curfew violations
- Personal appearance (generally hair and also inappropriate attire)

- Lack of responsibility
- Noncompliance around issues of Jewish observance
- And so forth and so on …

At this point, more often than not a huge cloud of silence descends upon the group as I stand in the front of the room patiently waiting for the bombshells that rarely fall without my prompting. "What about sex, drugs, and alcohol," I ask. "Not issues?" Oh yeah, those. We add them to the list. People like the workshop because it (a) reveals that they are not the only ones with the most obnoxious teenager in the world living in their home and (b) gives them hope that as the adults in the family, they can, perhaps with the help of others, get a grip on the situation.

When our oldest daughter was in middle school, I went to see the guidance counselor for reasons I can't quite remember now. Perhaps I had a foreshadowing of what was to come, with one adolescent in our home and two more in the pipeline. Here are the unforgettable words the counselor said to me in my search for comfort and reassurance: "There is nothing you can do to stop a teenager from doing what he or she wants to do. You can lock up the liquor, lock up the child, lock up the world, but a teen who wants to experiment with drugs, alcohol, or sex will do it no matter what you say or do." I was dumbfounded and skeptical. What losers her kids must be! I thought. I pictured my own family around the Shabbat dinner table, voices singing, faces glowing. My precious children would never do such things. I guess if they hadn't I wouldn't have written this book.

How do we deal with our Jewish teenagers when they are going in one direction and we want them to be going in another? How do we handle the (mostly) justifiable range of angry feelings that our teenagers inevitably evoke in us? How do we turn a caterer's check stuck on the refrigerator door into a moment of pride and triumph, or, if not that, how do we at least navigate the land mines of living with Jewish teens in a way that transforms us from tyrants into teachers?

The word *conflict,* according to the unabridged *Random House Dictionary of the English Language,* means "to come into collision or disagreement; be contradictory, at variance, or in opposition; clash."[3] For many parents of teens today, this definition might seem like the leitmotif, or recurring theme, of their family life. That teens want to have and do things we do not want them to have and do is not at all new—it is an extension of the usual parent-child encounter from the "terrible twos" on. What *is* new is that we are losing power and control and they are gaining it, both in terms of the natural process that occurs as children mature, and also as a result of some of the less healthy aspects of today's environment. Notes child development expert Dr. Mel Levine: "The balance of power seems to have shifted to children. Kids have a wealth of weapons at their disposal and parents have little leverage."[4] This makes for a very different and often difficult dynamic. How we move through these tumultuous moments can have an enduring impact on our relationships with our children into adulthood, and will affect them personally in ways too deep for us even to imagine. It is a challenge worth tackling.

In the best of cases, interpersonal conflicts can be peacefully resolved by clearly defining the problem, by posing alternative solutions, and by maintaining a respectful and forward-moving dialogue between the parties until an acceptable agreement is reached. In dealing with your teen, however, things are not always so simple, because all the issues of separation and control that we examined in Chapter 2 come heavily into play. For parents to be successful in negotiating conflicts with their teens, several other factors must be kept in mind, including expectations, appropriate use of authority, and love.

Examining Expectations

Sometimes conflict situations arise when we send our children mixed messages about what our expectations for them are, or when there is an actual clash between our expectations and theirs. In his work with synagogues around the country, Rabbi Richard Address of the Union for Reform Judaism's Department of Jewish Family

Concerns told me that parents often send unintended messages to their teens about what they really value. For example, when he asks parents what they think is most important for their teenagers to have in life, the parents are likely to say that they want their teens to grow up to become happy, decent human beings. When the children of these same parents are asked what they think their parents want for them, the teens typically answer, "To get high scores on the SATs so I can get into a top college."

> In a troubling *New York Magazine* article, Ralph Gardner observed, "The grueling competition has left teenagers, at an age when their idealism and sense of opportunity should be sparkling, cynical and pessimistic about their future. Rather than rejoicing in the freedom and adventure that college promised even a decade or two ago, they're worried about what's going to happen to them after they graduate." These and other fears amount to a palpable sense of threat—of social embarrassment through failure to live up to their own, their friends,' or their families' expectations.[5]

So in thinking about the expectations we have for our teens, it is important for us to think beyond the moment, in order to avoid putting pressures on them now that will result in unanticipated and unwanted outcomes in the future. In the haunting Harry Chapin ballad, "Cat's in the Cradle," for example, the always-working, unavailable father sends a message about "success" that his son adopts, with heartbreaking consequences for the father later on in life. The question is, what do we expect from our teens in the short term, and how do these expectations, and the accompanying pressures they carry, play out in the long term?

I always had trouble with the "pick your battles" parenting advice that on the surface seemed so wise. The problem was, I didn't know which battles to pick! When you are trying to get through the day-to-day and at the same time trying to prepare your teen for life beyond your home, things can get pretty complicated. The question of what kind of people we hope our children will become is one we rarely, if ever, ask ourselves, even though many of the expectations and pressures we place upon them flow from the unarticulated answer.

In thinking about the expectations we have and the battles worth fighting, it might be helpful to work through this exercise:

On an 8½" x 11" sheet of paper, make a chart with three columns. Label the first column, "I Expect My Teenager To ...." Label the second column, "Short-Range Implications of This Expectation," and label the third column "Long-Range Implications of This Expectation." Take some time and either alone or with your partner fill in the three columns.

In the first column, for example, you might say that you expect your teen to keep her room reasonably neat, and in the second column you might indicate that this has significant short-term implications because it affects everyone's mood, she is always complaining that she has nothing to wear and needs more money when in fact the money is invested in the clothing on the floor ... and so on. In terms of the longer-term implications, however, you might decide that this behavior is of no real consequence because when she has to live with others it will be resolved one way or another, or because it won't be your problem anymore(!), or whatever. On the other hand, a known or suspected use of drugs and/or alcohol may have serious short- and longer-term consequences. These would be particularly essential to note.

Now, put the chart aside, take a deep breath, and answer these questions in writing on the reverse side of the paper:

- What is the vision I have for my child when he is an adult?
- What do I picture her doing, what kind of person has she become? How does he treat himself and others, and what would others say about him?
- How do I want my child to remember me when I am gone?

Turn the paper over once again. Based on your deepest understanding of what really matters in life (i.e., your future vision rather than your present concerns about your teen), review what you have written in the three columns and decide, informed by your vision for the future, which things are worth fighting for. Put a check next to these in the third column and create a plan to address them. Use all the help you can find to do so. Family members and friends, parenting workshops, your rabbi, your pediatrician, a helpful guidance counselor, a therapist, books, articles, Internet resources—all of these are available to you as you search to craft an approach to articulating important expectations that will help your teen grow to be the best he or she can be.

Use of Authority

Sometimes we find ourselves in conflict with our teenager because the teen has initiated the situation, and sometimes it is we who must initiate a conflict situation. Our Jewish tradition offers us interesting perspectives in both scenarios.

a. When they initiate the conflict:

Anger, which may seem like such an appropriate response to some of the truly outrageous ways our teens at times act and speak, is actually discouraged by the famous twelfth-century scholar Maimonides:

> Anger is … an exceptionally bad quality. It is fitting and proper that one move away from it and adopt the opposite extreme. He should school himself not to become angry even when it is fitting to be angry. If he should wish to arouse fear in his children and household—or within the community, if he is a communal leader—and wishes to be angry at them to motivate them to return to the proper path, he should present an angry front to them to punish them, but he should be inwardly calm. He should be like one who acts out the part of an angry man in his wrath, but is not himself angry.

The early Sages said: Anyone who becomes angry is like one who worships idols. They also said: Whenever one becomes angry, if he is a wise man, his wisdom leaves him; if he is a prophet, his prophecy leaves him. The life of the irate is not [true] life.[6]

Sadly, I concur. If only I could go back in time and speak sternly to my teenagers when the occasion warranted, while feeling more in control of the situation than I actually was. Instead, I remember with great remorse moments of fury that only made matters worse.

Interestingly, however, there are odd parallels to my own loss of control in our sacred texts. On more than one occasion, God is so angry that God threatens to destroy humankind, and virtually does so in the story of Noah. At other times in the Torah, righteous leaders like Abraham and Moses intervene to save lives, with varying degrees of success. In the story of Sodom and Gomorrah, Abraham loses his bid to save the innocent because not even ten innocent adults could be found in that wicked place (Gen. 18:23–33, 19:23–25). Moses, on the other hand, does succeed in dissuading an angry God from wiping all the children of Israel off the face of the earth, when God wishes to start over and produce a less vexing group than the Israelites (Exod. 32:9–10). God, it seems, became enraged at the Israelites just as I had become enraged at my own children, so that can seem like a reassuring message on the one hand. On the other hand, however, the deeper message, as Maimonides makes clear, is that parents need to deal with the intensity of their anger in a way that will not be harmful or damaging to the other party.

I think the point is to reserve real anger for the extraordinarily few (hopefully never) moments that your child has behaved in a way that puts him or her in a category that approaches evil. But remember that, as we saw in Chapter 1, even a rebellious child whom the parents and the community agreed should be put to death never was. In the final analysis, a Jewish parent needs to keep working toward peace.

b. When (and why) we should initiate conflict:

Is there ever a time when a Jewish parent should initiate conflict with her teenager? Consider this text from the Torah: "You shall not hate your kinsfolk in your heart. Reprove your kin but incur no guilt on their account.... Love your fellow [Israelite] as yourself: I am the Lord" (Lev. 19:17–18). What does this text mean in terms of possible conflict between parents and teens? Commentators understand the essential meaning of this text to be that we are obligated to speak when we observe a fellow Jew committing a wrong. If we remain silent and do nothing to stop this person from doing wrong, so the thinking goes, we have, in effect, committed the wrong ourselves. In this sense, the idea of reproving or criticizing is to enable the other to grow, to improve, to become a better person. In modern terms, we might think of this as constructive feedback; in parent-child relations, we might think of it in terms of helping our children grow to be the best they can be, as this commentator suggests:

> You shall not hate your brother in your heart; you shall surely rebuke your neighbor.... What is the link between these two parts of the verse? The explanation is that one can only truly rebuke a person that one loves and whom one wishes to see mend his ways, such as the way a father rebukes his son. The closer a person is to another, the greater the love and the more earnest the rebuke. A rebuke which is the product of love is more effective.[7]

In other words, it continues to be our job as parents to provide constructive and loving criticism for our teens. How to do this in a way that will result in the least amount of conflict and resistance is not an easy feat, but this is nothing new, as this Talmud text indicates:

> Rabbi Tarfon said: "I wonder if there is anyone in this generation capable of accepting reproof.... Rabbi Elazar ben Azarya said: "I wonder whether there is anyone in this generation who knows how to reprove [without humiliating the one being criticized]" (BT, Arakhin 16b).

The message is that we as Jewish parents must struggle to communicate with our teenagers about important issues that will affect their welfare in a way that is caring and respectful, even when they least want to hear what we have to say.

Love

I truly believed that my daughter hated me. It was her senior year of high school, and I can hardly remember a civil conversation that took place between us at that time. And yet, for some unfathomable reason, I once asked her to meet me for lunch, and she, astonishingly, said yes. I wasn't sure why she agreed to do it, and I certainly didn't know what we would talk about, because it seemed as though we weren't on speaking terms, but she showed up. I'm sure there was conversation, though I don't know about what, and we decided to meet for lunch each week after that. Looking back on that time now, I can see that inside the angry, defiant teenager was a scared little girl who needed her mommy just to love her as she was.

Rick Warren, a Baptist minister whose writings and teachings have profoundly affected American churches of all denominations, has this to say about conflict: "When conflict is handled correctly, we grow closer to each other by facing and resolving our differences."[8] I would say that moments of conflict with our teenagers need to be balanced with moments of love. Sometimes the parent needs to take a time-out, to regroup and reconsider, to regain balance and perspective. Sometimes we need to smooth troubled waters by finding a "giveback," a peace offering of some kind. But mostly we need to be there, to stay in it, and to find ways in which we can say, "*Hineini,* I'm still here for you, and always will be."

5
Family Relationships

Family relationships evoke the widest possible range of human emotions, including love, need, dependence, pride, fear, and sometimes, tragically, even murderous rage. Family members can be our teachers and they can be our tormenters, and sometimes they are both. The biblical stories of our matriarchs and patriarchs send us this message loud and clear.

Despite all these apparent problems, families have always represented within Judaism the primary unit of life, the microstructure of our larger social order and the vehicle in which we travel through our time in this world. In fact, for Jews, family relationships do not even end with death, as we remember close family relations by saying the Kaddish prayer several times each year, until our own demise.[1]

The home in which a Jewish family dwells is supposed to reflect holiness, teaches Rabbi Menachem Mendl of Amishinov: "It is an obligation of every Jew to bring holiness into his/her private home, since the private life, the daily existence, and the atmosphere of the house should be saturated, full of holiness."[2] This description may seem like a stretch for many of us, but it does give us a window into a worldview that has shaped Jewish thinking—and Jewish living—for countless generations. Perhaps the message is that within our family units we have the potential for holiness, an opportunity to make choices that will make our world, and the world outside our doors, a better place.

For many of us, though, life doesn't seem to be going in that direction. We are finding it increasingly more difficult to connect as families and to offer meaningful help and support to one another as we move through life's day-to-day trials and challenges. For the families of today's teens, things are even more complicated. Here is how noted clinical psychologist Dr. Wendy Mogel, author of *The Blessing of a Skinned Knee,* describes the situation:

> A major complaint of adolescents is that nobody listens to them—and they may be right. The habit of listening, and of expecting to be listened to, needs to start early. If we are always distracted, always multitasking, our children will perceive us as half listening, and they'll stop trying to talk to us.... In communities of abundance, parents often try to fill their children's lives with "stuff": toys, tutors, and therapists. This happens, in part, because parents feel guilty about not spending enough time with their kids, so when their articulate, persuasive children lobby for goods and services, they give in. But ask any adult about his or her fondest early childhood memories, and you'll always hear the same thing: time spent with family, especially in nature or having an adventure, the smell and taste of favorite foods, the personality and warmth of a beloved relative.[3]

In previous chapters, we explored some of the enormous challenges facing today's Jewish families with teens. In this chapter, we will see how Jewish teachings about family relationships, particularly between parent and child, and siblings with one another, can enlighten and inspire us as we seek to maintain a sense of love, order, and sanity in a household that now contains that mysterious emerging adult we call a teenager.

(Jewish) Family Values

While this term has come to be associated with the political right-wing agenda, family values are nothing new. The Book of Genesis, the first book of the Torah, contains the meta-stories of our people told through family sagas that convey messages and meanings that remain compelling throughout the ages. On a superficial level, though, they don't always convey the kinds of values I personally would put on my "Ways in Which I Hope My Family Behaves" list. Here are three examples:

- Demonstrate your belief in God by agreeing to sacrifice the beloved only child of your wife's old age, but don't tell her you're doing it.

- Conspire with your favorite child to trick your ailing husband into giving your favorite child the blessing and birthright due his older brother, the child your husband prefers.

- If you can't stand your annoying sibling, gang up with your other siblings and sell him into slavery.

The first example is the famous story of the *akedah,* the binding of Isaac, which we read in synagogue on Rosh Hashanah. It's the story of God's call to Abraham, the first Jew: "Take your son, your favored one, Isaac, whom you love, and go to the land of Moriah, and offer him there as a burnt offering sacrifice"(Gen. 22:2). I love to study Jewish texts and reinterpret them in a way that can provide meaning and direction for our lives today, but I don't seem to be able to do that with this one. I think I would always choose my child. I struggle with this text every year, and I have yet to find peace in any of the explanations or interpretations I have ever come across. For me, it is one of those unyielding mysteries of Jewish life. I reluctantly accept that it is there and that it is part of our sacred story, and I move on. Come to think of it, sometimes it's like that in dealing with our teenagers, too. Maybe *that's* the message: there are times we have to accept what we can't understand about them, and just move on.

The second incident refers to Rebekah, whose beauty and kindness are noted in the famous drawing-water-at-the-well story (Gen. 24:16–19). Here she is, years later, involving her son in a deception against her ailing husband, as we noted in Chapter 2. At first glance, this is not a pretty sight. Digging a little deeper, though, we might find a touch of compassion for this woman who was married to a rather weak man (scarred, perhaps, by the fact that the father he adored was willing to slit his throat to show love for an unseeable God). Rebekah is mother to twin sons who are as different as they can be. At a Torah study discussion that my husband and I attended at a synagogue in Atlanta, a woman commented on the fact that when Rebekah was pregnant with these twin boys, God had specifically told her that "the older shall serve the younger" (Gen. 25:23). So maybe Rebekah spent her life trying to make real God's vision, despite all the on-the-ground difficulties that entailed. Perhaps that's the message here: there is a plan, and we must do our job to ensure that it works.

The third incident occurs in the story of Joseph and his brothers, whom we also met in Chapter 2. Joseph is the favored child of Jacob, who gives him a beautiful, multicolored coat. This serves to fuel even further Joseph's narcissistic dreams and fantasies about his superiority over his brothers, thereby driving them to the brink of fratricide. It's a story filled with drama, pain, and ultimate reconciliation, and it sets up the subsequent story of our people's enslavement in Egypt and our eventual redemption by a compassionate, caring God. I can't help but think, though, that there is a better way of bringing God's presence into the world than by a father causing such dysfunction and misery among his children. (In my own family, each of my children will say that I favor one of the others, when the truth is that each is my favorite in a love that defies logic or reason.) The message of the Joseph story, though, is not about love, it's about behavior: parents should not show clear favoritism to one child or another.

When we study Jewish texts about family relationships, we can't stop at a simple reading of the action and base serious conclusions on a superficial understanding of things as they appear at first glance. It's the same with our families, and especially with our teenagers. Beyond the behaviors and the moods of the moment lie nuances of feeling, emotion, conflict, and change. Just as we'll never completely understand the family stories of our Torah text no matter how long we go at it—there's no "end" of Torah study, except maybe death, though some mystics would say not even then—so maybe the message about our teens is: engage them with love, accept them as they are, look beyond the moment ("this too shall pass") and keep the door open for the next, hopefully positive, interaction.

Helpful Insights from Our Tradition

Family relationships, particularly those between parents and children, have long been a subject of great interest among the Rabbis of the Talmud as well as scholars and commentators to this very day. While the Torah gives the basic outlines and identifies the important principles—honor father and mother, for example—later codes were developed by Maimonides in the twelfth century, by Joseph Caro (*Code of Jewish Law*) in the sixteenth, and by others that contain specific instructions and formulations for the parent-child relationship. These make for truly fascinating reading and discussion, and though they are written from a patriarchal perspective, we can extend them to apply to females as well as males, where appropriate. Here are a few examples.

The Obligations of a Parent to His Child

According to the Babylonian Talmud, *Kiddushin* 29a, the obligations of a father to a son are:

- To circumcise him (i.e., enter him into the covenant)[4]
- To redeem him if he is a firstborn[5]
- To teach him Torah
- To take a wife for him
- To teach him a craft
- (and some say) To swim

For today's Jews, almost all the items on this list are astonishingly relevant, if we translate them into modern terms. To enter a male child into the covenant through the ceremony of brit milah or bris means to establish the boy's Jewish identity, to give him a Hebrew name, and to welcome him into the household of Israel. This is a joyous occasion, but not necessarily for the Jewish mother, for whom it can often be, as it was in my case, the beginning of endless anxiety about the baby's welfare, which for me continues to this day. Still, despite the initial assurances of the extremely tender, gentle, and sensitive mohel[6] ("We give the baby wine to suck, the nerve endings aren't really developed yet, he won't actually feel the pain...."), I was distressed. Finally, the mohel asked the ultimate question, "What choice do you have?" There you have it—there is no choice. If you want your baby boy to be a full member of the Jewish people, he gets circumcised.[7]

The obligation to teach a son Torah is pretty straightforward. The belief is that the study of Torah, including traditional commentaries and contemporary interpretations, teaches males and females alike how to live the most honest, the most ethical, and, ultimately, the most satisfying of lives, deeply connected to an eternal community that values every life as precious and unique. At its most basic level, the study of Torah is our ongoing connection to Jewish peoplehood, and being a part of the Jewish people is a blessing that Rabbi Shlomo Riskin describes this way:

> To be a Jew means to live in a universe of structure and purpose. To be a Jew means to feel part of a historic process guided by a God of love and concern and leading towards a world of peace and fulfillment. To be a Jew means to be a unique link in the great chain of Jewish being, to be crowned with the glory of majestic faith in freedom for all humanity, to be charged with the mission of imparting compassion and morality to an often insensitive and apathetic world. To be a Jew means to belong to a very special family within the family of nations, to relive that family's joys and tragedies, and to build one's future upon the experiences of the past. To be a Jew means to be together even in a society where so many are alone, to derive

security from deep roots even in a society where so many are struggling to merely remain afloat, to be inspired with significance even in a society where so many are bored and cynical.[8]

The next three obligations—to take a wife, teach him a craft, and teach him to swim—can be thought of in terms of "getting a life," (as our kids would say), and I think they apply equally to females and to males, just as most contemporary Jews would agree is the case with Torah study. We want to help our teenagers develop the values and the judgment that will enable them to make good decisions about life partners. We want to provide our teenagers with the learning they need to engage in work that will be satisfying to them, both financially and emotionally. (I always told my daughters that though I hoped they would have the opportunity to be stay-at-home moms when their children were little, I thought it was essential that they prepare for a profession that would ultimately be meaningful and that would enable them to be economically independent as well.)

And finally, teaching a child to swim had a very practical meaning when routes to the marketplace, the school, and places of commerce often involved crossing bodies of water: your ability to swim could literally save your life. Some rabbis have expanded the interpretation to mean teaching our children the skills and ways of being in the world that will enable them to survive in society.

Parents are also required to discipline their children and to teach them appropriate boundaries. To do this is seen as an act of love, and the reverse holds true: a parent who does not discipline his or her child does that child a great disservice. Here are two texts that illustrate the point.

> One must not occupy the place generally appointed for one's parent at the dinner table and one must not comment publicly on a statement made by one's parent when the parent is present, according to the Code of Jewish Law.[9]

> He who spares the rod hates his son, but he who loves him disciplines him early (Prov. 13:24).

Such sentiments may appear quite harsh to our modern sensibilities, especially the one from Proverbs. As we saw in Chapter 1, physical punishment is not considered an acceptable form of discipline in our culture today, though the Proverbs statement refers specifically to young children, and elsewhere we read: "If you strike a child, strike him only with a shoelace" (BT, *Bava Batra* 21a). This suggests to me that the purpose was more to get the child's attention than to cause physical pain. Interestingly, mental health professionals today are citing the many problems caused by overly permissive parenting, with its absence of strong limits, boundaries, and discipline. Consider this statement by Dr. Robert Kegan of Harvard University:

> As parents, we adults are called upon to set limits on behalf of a whole host of things that matter to us, not just preserving boundaries. In fact, one way we institute our vision, agenda, or overall plan for the family ... is by putting our foot down in the presence of anything that violates cherished elements of that vision. Our limit-setting may disappoint others and even enrage them—including especially the beloved others who may not only be members of our family but those on whose very behalf we are acting when we are disappointing and enraging them.[10]

Our tradition, it would seem, has gotten it right: the message is that to be a responsible parent, and surely to be a responsible Jewish parent, we must walk a difficult path to make sure our children understand that we mean what we say. With teens in particular, this is not always easy to do, and there is always the temptation to opt out. Reporting on a study of parent-teen relationships, a *USA Today* headline read: "Parents Want to Be Teen's Pals." The article cited parental unwillingness to discipline their teens and set appropriate limits for fear of incurring their children's anger and causing unhappiness.[11]

I actually knew parents like this when my children were teenagers, and I struggled mightily with feelings of jealousy and resentment toward them. My kids thought those parents were really cool, of course, and guess whose parents weren't. It's terribly painful when that little girl whose entire soul seemed to light up as you stepped through the door now can't seem to manage to say a civil word to you. You want her to love you again, maybe even like you again, but how can she when you are so mean to her, and all the other kids' parents let them … You can fill in the blank here. Setting appropriately strong boundaries and limits hurts a lot in the short run but brings blessing and appreciation to both parents and their teens in the long run. It was true back then, and it may even be more true for us today.

Jewish Parents as Role Models

Consider this tale about the Hasidic rabbi Ze'ev Wolf of Zhitomer:

> The Zhitomer rabbi was once walking along with his son when they saw a drunken man and his drunken son both stumbling into the gutter. "I envy that father," said the rabbi to his son. "He has accomplished his goal of having a son like himself. I don't know yet whether you will be like me. I can only hope that the drunkard is not more successful in training his son than I am with you."[12]

It's kind of frightening how, as they get older, our kids' behavior can remind us of our own worst qualities. This makes me think of the Torah text about the sins of the fathers being visited on the children (Exod. 34:6–7). There are many interpretations of this concept, but I think of it in a very personal and human way: our children are deeply influenced by what we do, whether they are ours through birth or adoption. We create their primary environment and we are their lifelong teachers, for better or for worse. By the time our children begin to move away from us in adolescence, the clay has been fashioned, even though we didn't create the original mold. These words from a High Holy Days prayer book are quite compelling in this regard: "Forgive us for condemning in our children the faults we tolerate in ourselves...."[13]

The point here is that we as parents should be constantly working on our own growth and improvement. In other words, if we want our children to be better, we have to work to be better ourselves. The process never stops. According to the creation story, God made the world "very good," but not perfect. There is room for us to make things better—in our world, and in our families.

Sibling Rivalry

This is a big theme in the Book of Genesis, the part of the Torah that deals most directly with family relationships, and it's a big theme in family life. The message of the three following texts would seem to be that parents can avoid sibling rivalry through their own actions:

> Love equally all your children. Sometimes the favored disappoint, and the neglected make you happy" (Berekiah Ha-Nakdan, *Mishle Shualim,* 1260 CE).[14]

> Play no favoritism: Because Joseph got a multicolored coat, the brothers "hated him" (Rabbi Eleazar ben Azariah, Genesis *Rabbah* 84:8).[15]

> Each child carries its own blessing into the world (Yiddish proverb).[16]

However, noted therapist and author Rabbi Abraham J. Twerski, who has worked extensively with Jews in recovery from chemical and other dependencies, suggests that sibling rivalry is a dimension of the human condition and only minimally subject, if at all, to the behavior of parents:

> Resentment toward a younger sibling does not necessarily require a rational basis. Or to put it another way, the threat of loss of parental attention and the need to share parental love with someone else is a rational basis for resentment. At any rate, such resentment may occur even when there are abundant resources for children.[17]

Of all the things my children did to one another that really bothered me, I found *lashon hara* to be the most intolerable. The term *lashon hara* literally means "evil" or "wicked tongue," and it refers to the infinite number of ways we human beings devise to hurt or belittle one another. Actions that classify as *lashon hara* range from the seemingly innocuous ("Did you hear that Josh Klein got into Yale? I heard he wasn't such a great student. Maybe his parents gave a big gift ...") to outright, overt, destructive gossip ("I heard Mimi Fuchs got that promotion because she really knows how to please her boss, if you know what I mean ..."). Even telling the plain, unedited truth can be *lashon hara* if it needlessly causes shame, embarrassment, or discomfort to another. Our rabbis have always railed against *lashon hara,* and for good reason: this mean-spirited behavior wounds others and at some level undermines the peace of the community.

Three siblings can be a lot more lethal than two in this regard because any two of them can work in tandem to demolish the third: one makes the cruel statement, and the second affirms it. And siblings have an unnerving ability to sense each other's most vulnerable spots. It's where they are most likely to take aim. It hurt me terribly to hear my emerging adolescent children harming and undermining each other, when I thought that instead they should be helping each other deal with the meanness of cliques and the other challenges that lay outside our home. I was therefore determined to put an end to *lashon hara,* and I tried a variety of methods.

First, I instituted a fine for name-calling or making insulting remarks. The fine went into the *tzedakah* (charity) box we kept in our kitchen, the hub of our Jewish family life. There were a number of problems with this approach: I couldn't verify insults that I hadn't myself heard, and this made the victim angry; and I realized that giving the money to charity wasn't as meaningful as it would be to give it to the victim. If Child A has to pay compensation to Child B for unkind words said, I reasoned, Child A will be less likely to do it because he/she won't want Child B to profit in any way. Wrong! I upped the ante fourfold. The result? The transgressor would come to me with a gleeful smile, wave the money in front of my face, pro-claiming, "It's worth it," and then insult and pay the victim.

Have I mentioned that my kids are more clever than I am?

Finally, I devised a solution that gives me pleasure to think of even to this day. In one of the Judaica bookstores where I love to browse, I came across a volume called *Guard Your Tongue: A Practical Guide to the Laws of Loshon Hora,* adapted from teachings of the Chofez Chaim.[18] We are talking about roughly two hundred pages of instructions and prohibitions on this subject. I purchased the book and placed it on the large center island in our kitchen. When-ever I overheard malicious, hurtful words directed at one child by another, the offender was required to sit in the kitchen, open the book to any page, and read it out loud.

Did this have the desired effect? I truly can't know for sure, though looking back, maybe it did, since the reading eventually ceased. Did my children learn anything from the words they were reading? I don't know, but I sure did, and I found the experience to be quite a blessing in that respect.

There are many tales of the destructive power of sibling rivalry, but there can be beauty and sweetness in sibling relationships as well. In the Torah, Miriam had initiated a jealous conversation with her brother Aaron against their brother Moses. God, furious, pun-ished Miriam by striking her with a leprosy-like skin disease, and Aaron begged Moses to intercede. So in a deeply moving plea on behalf of the sister who had spoken against him, Moses cried out to God, "O God, please heal her!" (Num. 12:10–13).

Although there are no foolproof formulas about how to achieve harmonious sibling relationships, here are the conclusions I have reached about parental responsibility in this area:

- Avoid comparisons. This is deadly stuff—no exaggeration. Just look at the story of Cain and Abel in the Bible. Cain kills his brother Abel because God, the heavenly parent, prefers Abel's offering to the offering that Cain brings (Gen. 4:3–8). Don't compare one child to another, and don't even give news reports about one child to another. This is true when they are little, when they are teens, and throughout their lives.

- Focus on uniqueness. Psychologists tell us that children don't need to be treated equally; they need to be treated according to their individual needs. This means you actually have to know your child very well and respond appropriately. Many believe that the model of the four children in the Passover Haggadah sends us this message loud and clear, as we will see later in this chapter.

- Articulate your appreciation. Don't hold back! Pay attention to your teen's efforts and accomplishments, and praise whenever it is appropriate to do so. (There were times when I felt that giving my teen a standing ovation for getting out of bed before noon during a school vacation might be in order, but this is not quite what I mean here.) Each child/teen needs to know that you care and that you appreciate the good things he or she does.

- Devote adequate time to each child. This can be so terribly difficult when children are teenagers and it seems that they don't want to spend a second of free time with you! Trust me, they still know you are there. An older teen will see you spending time with a younger sibling in a way that may make him feel jealous, even if he doesn't want to be with you himself. One way to let the more elusive teen know that you still care is to leave an occasional handwritten note or letter. No criticism or reminders about chores—this is a love note.

- Have realistic expectations. The Torah is full of stories of unresolved sibling rivalry,[19] so don't drive yourself crazy with this. You won't be able to make sibling rivalry go away. Parents have a responsibility, however, to make their home as safe an environment as possible, so you do have to step in if one child is victimizing another.

- Listen with your heart. You can't agree or disagree with one child's general complaints about another—trust me, it will come back to bite you in the end. The best you can do is listen, affirm that there are differences and stresses in every family, and express the hope that the children will be mature enough to work things out, if not now, then at least in the future.

Finally, modeling good behavior with our own family members—brothers and sisters, and parents if we have them—teaches our children more about how to treat their siblings than any of our words could ever do.

Tips for Parenting Jewish Teens from a Well-Known Source

How do we actually take the lessons of our tradition and transform them into parenting actions in our daily lives? We have looked at some Jewish values and interpreted their meanings and messages for our time. But are there things that make sense for us and that we can actually *do,* based on the wisdom of our tradition? If you are among the 80 percent of American Jews who attend a Passover seder each year, you have already held in your hands an extraordinary tool that can help you do just that. It's called the Passover Haggadah.

The word *Haggadah* is derived from the Hebrew word that means "to tell." The purpose of the Passover Haggadah is to move us through the telling of our people's master story from slavery to freedom. The Torah commands us to do this: "And when, in time to come, your son asks you, saying, 'What does this mean?' you shall say to him, 'It was with a mighty hand that Adonai brought us out from Egypt, the house of bondage'" (Exod. 13:14). Within the context of the Passover seder, the Haggadah represents a teaching vehicle par excellence, as it fosters questions and answers between parents and children.

The first printed version of the Haggadah dates to about the late fifteenth century, with handwritten manuscripts in existence long before then. Today, there are more than four thousand versions of published Haggadot (pl.), reflecting a wide range of orientations, tastes, and preferences in dozens of languages. This number does not include, of course, the countless Haggadot created by individuals and families for their own personal use. The Haggadah, it would seem, holds a uniquely important place in the heart of the Jewish people, despite differences in religious observance, cultural orientation, and nation of domicile. Because its core elements remain the same even as Jews adapt it to their own needs in their own time, the Haggadah reflects the genius of Jewish survival. It's a great resource guide for the parents of Jewish teens.

What the Haggadah Can Teach Us about Parenting Jewish Teens

The chart on the following page titled "Some Lessons the Haggadah Can Teach the Parents of Jewish Teens" presents an overview of how aspects of the Haggadah can help us improve our parenting. Here's how it works: Just as the headings suggest, each row cites an element in the Haggadah (column #1), the value it expresses (column #2), a corresponding lesson for parents of Jewish teens (column #3), and a column called "How I Can Apply It," which is blank. By reading across each row, you can make the connections between the Haggadah and an action that you can apply to your own parenting. If you have a spouse, a partner, an adult family member, or a close friend with whom to work through these issues, that would be ideal. In any case, it is entirely possible to do this on your own, and you will literally be transforming the teachings of our tradition into your own life—the power to do so is in your hands.

Here's an example of how I would use this chart, based on our family's experiences and particular situation. In the first row across, I would give serious thought to the lesson, "Respectful communication between the generations is essential." I would apply the lesson by listing actions I could take to make this happen, which might go something like this:

Some Lessons the Haggadah Can Teach
the Parents of Jewish Teens

In the Haggadah	The Value This Expresses	The Lesson for Parents of Jewish Teens	How I Can Apply It
Intergenerational dialogue and interaction are encouraged.	The engagement of our children is a priority.	Respectful communication between the generations is essential.	
The model of four types of children is presented.	Every individual must be treated in an appropriate way.	Attention to the individual (and changing) needs of our teens is vital.	
We are reminded of the experience of slavery.	We should treat others as we would like to be treated.	Even when we disagree, we should strive to behave respectfully.	
We are guided through the seder in a specific order.	There is a specific, correct way to doing certain things.	There are some issues and values about which compromise may not be desirable or appropriate.	
We acknowledge the suffering of our enemies.	It is always important to behave with some degree of compassion.	We should be sensitive and caring when we must make decisions that may cause our teen pain.	
The bread of slavery becomes the symbol of freedom.	The capacity exists for transforming problems into opportunities.	We can help our teens become more resilient by working with them toward mutually satisfactory outcomes.	
We look forward to being in Jerusalem next year.	Hope is a hallmark of the Jewish people.	In the most difficult moments, we need to reassure our teen that better days lie ahead.	

1. We agree upon a mutually convenient time to discuss an impor-
   tant/serious issue. For example, "Let's meet at 7:30 tonight to
   establish a policy about what is appropriate attire for school."

2. We establish ground rules for the conversation. For example,
   you can speak without interruption from me, and I can then
   speak without interruption from you. We might want to establish a time limit for each speaker.

3. We will then state, or perhaps write, the disagreement as we
   understand it.

4. We will determine whether there is anything in our separate
   positions that we might be able to agree upon. For example, I
   care what my friends (community) think of me, and the actions
   of my family have an impact on that; you care what your friends
   think of you, and the actions of your family have an impact on
   that. Bingo! We both acknowledge caring what the outside
   world thinks of us and our family.

5. We can then, separately or together, develop two or three scenarios for the resolution of the problem and try to work
   through them. It is important to note that we will *try* to work
   through them; respectful dialogue does not always mean that
   both parties will be satisfied with the outcome, especially in par-
   ent/teen relationships. What it does mean is that both parties
   will be treated with respect in presenting and explaining their
   point of view.

A Few Words about the Four Sons/Children

The Haggadah describes four types of children (commonly translated as "sons" but the Hebrew could mean "children" as well, and
that is the way I will refer to it). These prototypes were developed in
the Midrash, a collection of rabbinic stories and commentaries,
based on several verses in the Torah.[20]

> The wise child asks, "What is the meaning of the testimonies,
> statutes, and judgments which the Eternal our God has

commanded us?" You shall explain to him all the laws of Passover, to the very last detail about the *afikomen.*

The wicked child asks: "What is the meaning of this service to you!" Saying *you,* he excludes himself, and because he excludes himself from the group, he denies a basic principle of our faith. You in turn should set his teeth on edge and say to him: "Because of what the Eternal did for me when I came forth from Egypt" I do this. For *me* and not for *him;* had he been there, he would not have been redeemed.

The simple child asks: "What is this?" To him you shall say: "With a strong hand the Eternal brought us out of Egypt, from the house of bondage."

As for the child who does not even know how to ask a question, you must begin for him, as it is written in the Bible: "You shall tell your child on that day: 'This is done because of that which the Eternal did for me when I came forth out of Egypt.' "[21]

Many fascinating interpretations of this model of the four children can be found. Some say that it is all the same child, with different moods and perhaps at different developmental stages. Others say that maybe different learning styles are represented here and that it is incumbent on parents to respond appropriately. A rather unique interpretation sees in this model four generations of one family:

One interpretation: four generations of the same family. The Wise Son is the grandfather, the classical observant Jew. The Wicked Son is the next generation, who grew up in an observant home, but who abandoned it all. He tries to provoke his father's generation by asking, "What does this all mean to you?" thereby distancing himself. The Simple Son is the third generation; his father rebelled against the observant grandfather. He is surprised when he sees the difference between his father's and his grandfather's homes, and doesn't know what to make of it all. The Son Who Does Not Know to Ask is the fourth generation. His great-grandfather, the observant Jew, has died, and this son is born totally ignorant and doesn't know what to ask. "He, of all the sons, has the best chance of returning to his roots. It is not the Simple Son, and certainly not the Wicked Son, but the one who does not know how to ask, who will come full circle."[22]

This commentary struck me as rather surprising, yet when I thought more about it, it seemed to describe my own situation quite well. Having had virtually no Jewish observance in the home in which I grew up, I think I was more positive about exploring Judaism as an adult than were adults who had experienced their earlier Jewish education and observance as a meaningless series of restraints and restrictions from which they longed to be free. Even so, I wouldn't count on a return to Judaism like my own happening in big numbers. Instead, I believe we should work toward building within our own homes a way in which Judaism can be a positive, lived experience for everyone in the family.

I think the model of the four children, with its wide range of possible interpretations, holds a special message for the parents of Jewish teens, and it is this: never is the wicked child banished from the table. How remarkable this is! No matter how strong the condemnation of that child may be, he or she is never asked to leave the group, even though the child has expressed alienation from the family and its customs and practices. This reminds me of a Talmud verse that originally referred to the exile of the Jewish people, but that conveys a deep poignancy when applied to parenting teens:

> Alas for the children who are exiled from their parents' table.
> Alas for the parents who have exiled their children (adapted from Berachot 3a).

I think the message is clearly this: Jewish parents must not reject their children. We must figure out how to live with them, even when they seem to reject *our* values and beliefs. Never give up on your child is how we can read these texts.

Spiritual Guidance

In the countless arguments I've had with my children over the years about issues too numerous to mention, I have found myself articulating and holding to positions that sometimes defied logical explanation, but that somehow resonated deep within my soul, as if my blessed ancestors were calling out to me from their heavenly synagogue or coffee klatch: "Joanne! Don't let her do that! Joanne! Say no to him!" It is not a good idea to try to explain this method of decision making to today's teenagers.

I have felt that there is something deeper to parenting our teens than what is offered by the often informative, but spiritually empty, popular books on the subject. There is, perhaps, a dimension to being a Jewish parent that cannot be defined, a nonrational connection to all those who came before us and a sense of responsibility to those who will follow. This feeling can play itself out in very concrete ways.

In the middle of our eldest daughter's junior year of high school, she began what might be called The Campaign for Complete Post-Prom Freedom. This entailed permission to engage in the custom of renting a beach house on the Jersey shore and crashing there for several days immediately following the senior prom. We argued about this for literally over a year. Jen, being no fool, realized that by prom time she would be eighteen and therefore legally free to do whatever she wanted without our permission. To her credit, she saved this trump card until all else failed.

"Mom, if you believe that I won't get involved in dangerous behaviors there, if you believe that I won't be getting drunk, taking drugs, and other stuff, why won't you just say yes?"

I couldn't really answer her question, so I just said no.

Finally: "Mom, you know I'm going to be eighteen and I don't really need your permission to go. I'd like to have it, but I don't need it, and I'm going with my friends no matter what you say."

By now the ancestors in my head had turned up the volume on the muttering and head shaking, so I said, "Jen, you're right, you can go if you choose to. I can't stop you. I don't even have a rational reason to give you for saying no. I believe in you, and I trust you to take good care of yourself. All I can say is that this Jewish mother cannot feel okay about this lovely Jewish daughter spending a weekend in an environment like that. It's as simple and as irrational as that." In the silence that followed, I suppose we each struggled with the values we had learned and the experiences we had shared, she from her perspective and me from mine. After some time, she said, "I understand what you are saying," and she left the room. Months later, the post-prom beach house party went on as scheduled, but without our precious daughter. She attended the supervised school-sponsored event instead.

Thank God.

6

Jewish Observance: Yours, Mine, and Ours

It was Friday night. Aaron was standing at the door of our bedroom waiting for an answer. Ron and I were huddled in the corner like two major-league coaches getting ready to call the big play. Should we let our fifteen-year-old son sleep over at a friend's house after Shabbat dinner? What were the rules for his older sisters when they were his age? Did Aaron finish his science project yet? Will the parents be at home? Who else will be there? Why doesn't he invite his friends to come over here instead?

"Uh, Mom? Dad? Hello?"

Working through issues of Jewish observance becomes especially tricky for many families when the sweet little children who used to sit with scrubbed faces around the joyous Shabbat dinner table turn into awkward, grungy adolescents who'd rather be out cruising the wide, wide world with their friends than at home with their boring parents. In this chapter, we will explore the question of why and how to maintain Jewish observance with less-than-enthusiastic teenagers in the home. Our consideration of Jewish observance will focus specifically on Shabbat and holidays, synagogue attendance, and formal Jewish education. Finally, we will examine "Yours, Mine, and Ours" approaches designed to facilitate peace in the home with teenagers present. If you are not involved in any of these activities, don't skip this chapter! You may learn something you can apply to other areas of parenting Jewish teens, and who knows? Maybe you'll learn something new about Jewish family life with teens that will appeal to you.

Jewish Observance—Why Bother?

I think there are many reasons for choosing to live a Jewish life. Here are the three I hear the most:

1. We are commanded to do so by God, as explained in the Torah and in later sacred writings and teachings.
2. The Holocaust and other attempts to destroy the Jewish people have decimated our numbers and we are obligated to keep Judaism alive.
3. It's the best possible road map for our journey through this world (and, some would say, the next).

In my opinion, these are all good and valid reasons for choosing to live a Jewish life, and they are not mutually exclusive: it is possible to hold to one, two, or all three positions, and others as well. For the purposes of our investigation here, though, we will focus on the third one—it's the best possible road map for our journey through this world. What, precisely, does this mean?

Rereading the Shema

Virtually all Jews know the Shema proclamation as the watchword of the Jewish faith: *Shema Yisrael, Adonai Eloheinu, Adonai Echad*— Hear O Israel, Adonai is our God, Adonai is One. We learn it in early childhood, it is said at the morning and evening synagogue services, and we are supposed to recite it at night before going off to sleep. Some say that these should be our very last words in this life, to be uttered immediately before taking our final breath. What some Jews may not know is that the proclamation is actually part of a larger rubric that contains biblical verses both before and after (Deut. 6:4–9 and 11:13–21 and Num. 15:37–41). For now, we are most interested in these:

> If, then, you obey the commandments that I enjoin upon you this day, loving Adonai your God and serving Adonai with all your heart and soul, I will grant the rain for your land in season, the early rain and the late. You shall gather in your new grain and wine and oil—I will also provide grass in the fields for your cattle—and thus you shall eat your fill. Take care not to be lured away to serve other gods and bow to them. For Adonai's anger will flare up against you, shutting up the skies so that there will be no rain and the ground will not yield its produce; and you will soon perish from the good land that Adonai is assigning to you (Deut. 11:13–17).[1]

At first glance, or even second, third, or fourth, this text may not seem to be speaking to us today in any compelling way. It basically reads like a threat to farmers who lived a long time ago—if you obey God you'll get what you need for a good crop and if you don't obey God, you'll starve to death. Students and teachers of Torah call these "blessings and curses," and they appear, sometimes in different forms, several times in the Torah. Since I'm not a farmer and I don't have a field in need of rain, I might be tempted to think of this text as irrelevant, and if a text surrounding the Shema is irrelevant … well, you can see where this might be going.

However, we can think about blessings and curses in more modern terms. Up close and personal, we see increasing amounts of sexual activity among today's younger teens and preteens, rising incidences of eating disorders and self-destructive teen behaviors, high rates of depression among our young people, and escalating violence and bullying that occurs in middle schools and high schools.

I can't really say that I believe there is a direct connection between being an observant Jew (however you understand that term) and the avoidance of all these "curses." What I *do* believe is that the choice we Jewish adults make about whether or not to bring ourselves into a caring community of Jews affects how supported—or how lonely—we will be as we struggle with life's most painful moments and celebrate its most joyous ones. Rabbi Shlomo

Riskin's description of what I would call the "benefits of membership" in the Jewish community appears in Chapter 5 on page 46 and is worth rereading. For American Jews today, membership in the Jewish community reaches its fullest level of potential with the intersection of these three points: Jewish home observance, active synagogue affiliation, and Jewish education or ongoing Jewish learning. Before exploring these, let's consider the possible terms of engagement for families with teens.

Jewish Observance with Teens

For some parents, this phrase may seem like an oxymoron. My observation has been that most non–Orthodox teens (and many Orthodox ones as well) are not particularly enthralled with the practices of Jewish observance, even if they were when they were younger. This being the case, there are three basic choices that can be made:

- You can give up on Jewish observance.
- You can exile your child from the table.
- You can make accommodations that parents and teens can live with.

Here is my short-form commentary on these:

Giving up on Jewish observance doesn't really buy you anything. Your kids won't love you more for it, though they may swear that they will, and you will have lost a connection that might have sustained you through difficult times and gladdened your heart during happy ones. My advice: show your teens your own stability and stick with it. Teenage aliens do have a habit of returning from outer space in their twenties, and some have actually been known to return to the ways of their parents' teachings when they themselves become parents. I don't recommend giving up.

Exiling your teen from the table because of his or her rebellion against your family's observance may relieve a great source of irritation in the short run, but it may prove quite costly later on. There are multiple ways of reading and interpreting our classical Jewish texts, and there is one that we encountered earlier that seems especially poignant and compelling to me in this connection. Although it was originally intended to refer to God's exiling the Jewish people from the Land of Israel, the Talmud text that reads, "Alas for the children who are exiled from their parents' table /Alas for the parents who have exiled their children," can be understood, I believe, as a metaphor for our own relationship with our children. Exiling your teen physically, emotionally, or both, should be avoided at all costs. Finally, consider this opinion:

> A story is told about the Ba'al Shem Tov ("Master of the Good Name"), the founder of Hasidism. A man once complained to him that his son had turned completely away from religion. "What shall I do, Rebbe?" the distraught man pleaded. "Do you love your son?" the Ba'al Shem Tov asked. "Of course I do." "Then love him even more."[2]

I rest my case.

My recommendation is to take the middle ground: Jewish parents, with the help of their teens, must fashion a strategy for living together under these transitional conditions. This approach, I believe, has the highest probability of turning out to be a win-win situation in the long run. Later in this chapter we will explore specific suggestions for how you might accomplish this. For now, though, let's turn to the specific issues we will be addressing: Shabbat, holiday observance, synagogue attendance, and Jewish education/lifelong Jewish learning.

Before we proceed, it is important to say a word or two about what I mean by "Jewish observance." Of course, there is a wide range of possibilities implied in this term, especially in twenty-first-century America. For our purposes, however, Jewish observance does not mean Jewish values, beliefs, ethics, personal feelings of identity, and the like. These are all good and important things, but they are not the topics of this chapter. Adherence to the Jewish dietary laws (kashrut), also an important aspect of Jewish observance because it permeates the consciousness of being Jewish on a 24/7 basis, will not be included here either.

The Sabbath

What is the Sabbath and why is it important?

Plain and simple, the Sabbath is a day of holy rest. According to the Torah, God created heaven and earth and "all their array" in six days of work and on the seventh day God ceased from work, blessed the seventh day, and called it holy (Gen. 2:1–3). We are commanded to rest on the seventh day as well, for a twenty-five–hour period that begins at sundown on Friday and ends Saturday evening. Resting on the Sabbath is important because:

- We are emulating God's behavior and opening ourselves up to experiencing that which is holy.

- It is a quintessentially Jewish thing to do and on some level connects us at least once a week to Jews of generations past, to those of generations in the future, and to Jews around the world today.

- It provides us with the opportunity to renew ourselves and to engage with our family, our friends, and our community in a way that is not possible during the regular workweek.

Consider this image:

On Friday evening, a white cloth covers the table, and on it are the best dishes and silver, two loaves of challah under a beautiful covering, a Kiddush cup filled with wine, and a bouquet of flowers. The home is filled with the tantalizing aroma of a delicious meal. The family gathers. *Tzedakah* is placed in a special container to be given to a charity at a later time, the mother (traditionally) lights and blesses the Sabbath candles, and the parents bless the children.

Other blessings and rituals follow and the family is seated for feasting, talking, and sharing without the distractions of cell phones, iPods, television, and instant messages.

Now consider this:

> Study after study finds that kids who eat dinner with their families regularly are better students, healthier people and less likely to smoke, drink or use drugs than those who don't. A University of Michigan study of children ages 3 through 12, for example, found that more meal time with the family was the single strongest predictor of better achievement scores and fewer behavioral problems—even better than time spent studying or in church. Bill Doherty, a professor of family social science at the University of Minnesota says: "Make it special. Light candles, put a tablecloth out. Distinguish between a routine and a ritual."[3]

It's always nice when the rest of the world affirms the ideas we have been working with since Mount Sinai.

For years, Shabbat was an organizing principle in the life of our family. Friday evenings were predictably sweet in our home, as we shut out the distractions of the world and became reacquainted with one another. After lighting the Shabbat candles, my husband and I would bless our children, Ron with English words from his heart and me with some approximation of the traditional Hebrew blessings. At the dinner table, we would ask each person present to share with the rest of us the sweetest or the nicest thing that had happened to him or her that week. It is amazing how focusing on something positive can transform a bad mood into a better one.

At some point, however, into this lovely Friday-evening Sabbath experience began to seep the angst and the oppositional behavior of the teenage years. Things got so bad that, I'm embarrassed to admit, there were moments when I actually dreaded gathering around the table with the family. One Friday evening in particular, after a week of especially contentious fighting between one of the children and me, I was filled with anxiety as I lit the Sabbath candles and sang the blessing to the background sounds of exaggerated sighs of impatience and attempts to engage the other siblings in distracting conversation. When I finished, I turned to bless the children and I (consciously or unconsciously) skipped that one. Stunned, she grabbed my hands and placed them on her head, crying: "Bless me, Mommy, bless me, too!" In that moment I glimpsed the importance of holding fast to the values and practices that Jewish parents teach their children, even when as teenagers they seem to hate you for them.

Holiday Celebrations

Jewish holiday preparation and celebration can have a unifying and renewing effect on parents and teens, even during periods that are otherwise stressful or challenging. Jewish holiday observances help us mark time through the cycle of the year in a particularly Jewish way, and warm memories of holidays past can have a restorative effect on family relationships in the present. It is important that we acknowledge, at least to ourselves, that today's teen is no longer yesterday's child, and the holiday observance will therefore be different than it was in the past.

One year, my husband tried to bring order to my legendary anxiety about pre-Passover cleaning, shopping, and cooking by creating a "Passover To-Do List" on one of our early home computers. The list was two pages long, and I started hyperventilating the first time I saw it. Ron immediately called the family together and led us through the process of selecting/assigning each task. This leadership on his part had two important benefits: (1) it transformed an overwhelming process into a series of discrete, manageable tasks, and (2) it created a family holiday-preparation record that we updated each year, and that even to this day evokes the deepest feelings of nostalgia and loving memory, as we remember who chopped the walnuts and who peeled the apples for the *charoset* in any given year. Drawing upon the sweet memories of holidays past can have a calming effect as we negotiate with our teens in the more tumultuous present.

Here is a sampling of ideas you may find helpful in fashioning observances that will work for your teen in celebrating some of the Jewish holidays:

- High Holy Days—Beyond the obligatory synagogue attendance on Rosh Hashanah and Yom Kippur, parents and teens can use the holiday theme of *teshuvah,* repentance, to identify behaviors that need to change for both personal and family well-being. Avoid creating a laundry list here; instead, earnestly search for one improvement and a commitment to strive for it. Parents can help teens by taking the first step and acknowledging a parental behavior that needs changing—this kind of courageous self-assessment is invaluable modeling for teens.

- Sukkot—Practically the first thing we did when we moved from Manhattan to the suburbs was to purchase a sukkah, the representation of the temporary hut our ancestors dwelled in during the fall harvest season long ago. Jews construct and "dwell in" the sukkah (i.e., take our meals there, sleep there, or both) during the holiday of Sukkot. Even when our children were teens, the fun of meals in the sukkah remained. Conversations in that setting can easily turn to the important life questions of fragility and vulnerability, which are themes of this holiday and have great relevance for teens. Thankfulness for the abundance we enjoy and plans to help others less fortunate than us are also appropriate topics for the Sukkot holiday.

- Hanukkah—Our children enjoyed receiving gifts on each of the eight nights of Hanukkah until they went off to college, but we introduced the concept of a "gift of love" for at least one of those nights. That gift involved something that was negligible in terms of financial cost but that had relationship value, such as lunch alone with Mom or Dad on the next family vacation, an otherwise-prohibited school-night sleepover, or a "your choice" of time to be spent together. Playing "high stakes" dreidel with teens can be family fun in a way you might never have imagined when they were younger, so give it a try!

- Purim—One of the three commandments regarding Purim observance is to give gifts of food to friends and *tzedakah* (charity) to the poor. Besides the fun of baking (or buying) and eating hamantaschen, Purim provides a great opportunity for teens to commit to engaging in projects that combat poverty. On the other hand, I think it is important to note that the custom of getting so drunk on Purim that we can't distinguish between the name of Mordechai, the hero, and Haman, the villain, should be handled extremely carefully in the presence of teens.

- Passover—The Passover seder represents a quintessential intergenerational learning and sharing experience. Consider assigning your teenager the responsibility for finding additional readings and commentaries, modern or traditional, so that he or she can lead a discussion during the meal about a relevant topic that interests a person of that age.

Involving your teen in the holiday planning and celebration process can help maintain and strengthen an important bond of Jewish family life, even as your family grows and changes over time.

Synagogue Attendance

It was a cold Saturday night in January. My husband and I had agreed to take Aaron, then eight, to Sports and Games after Shabbat was over. Sports and Games was one of those huge indoor play parks filled with video games, skeet bowling, batting cages, and other assorted distractions for the mostly males-of-all-ages set. This was a reward to Aaron for surviving the Sabbath day in our home, which meant lots of hugs and family time, but no television or computers.

I came prepared. I brought a book. As soon as we entered the aircraft-hangar-like space, I made my way to the snack area and sat down at a table with a cup of coffee. I let my husband, Ron, go off with our son and felt quite justified in doing so. After all, hadn't I done all the necessaries with the two older sisters?

I put my nose in the book, but there was no drowning out the environment. I experienced a serious level of irritation every time I entered this place, and that night was no exception. I reflected on my feelings: I found the people uninteresting and irrelevant, I hated the sounds and noises that surrounded me, and I resented wasting my time in this utterly meaningless place. Dear God, I thought with the shock of revelation, this is exactly how our teenagers feel in the synagogue.

After bar/bat mitzvah, many teenagers catch a kind of wanderlust that makes them want to go everywhere—except the synagogue! On the one hand, I understood how they felt after that moment of revelation at Sports and Games; on the other hand, it was one of those values my husband and I couldn't give up completely. We therefore developed the "Once-a-Month-No-Arguments" peace plan, which I heartily recommend to you. The basic provision of the plan allows the teen to choose a minimum of one Friday night or Saturday morning a month to attend, but without any arguments. We worked and reworked the plan over the years that we had teenagers living in our home, and it was truly never a perfect solution. Still, sometimes, we just do the best we can and hope for the best possible outcome under the circumstances while we look forward to the time when our children will find, on their own terms, meaning and purpose within the sanctuary of the synagogue community.

Jewish Education/Lifelong Jewish Learning

When I'm leading workshops, I often ask participants at what point they think a Jewish parent stops being a teacher to his or her children. After some conversation, the inevitable response is, "Not until you die." Recently, however, a man in the group added: "Not even then."

Jewish parents are obligated to teach their children, and the lessons we learn from our parents, for better or for worse, live on in us even after our parents are gone. The injunction to be a teacher to one's child is quite explicit:

> Therefore impress these My words upon your very heart: bind them as a sign on your hand and let them serve as a symbol on

your forehead, and teach them to your children—reciting them when you stay at home and when you are away, when you lie down and when you get up; and inscribe them on the doorposts of your house and on your gates—to the end that you and your children may endure, in the land that the Lord swore to your fathers to assign to them, as long as there is a heaven over the earth (Deut. 11:18–21).

The words that we are supposed to teach our children are the words of the Torah, and we are to do this everywhere (at home and away) and all the time (when we end the day and when we begin it). In other words, the job of a Jewish parent is to teach Torah constantly to his or her children because the study of Torah will lead to a life filled with purpose and meaning and the performance of deeds of loving-kindness.

Though we are obligated to provide this learning, most of us aren't equipped to homeschool our children in Hebrew and Jewish studies, so we send them to Hebrew school, religious school, or Jewish day school for their formal Jewish education. The truth is, though, that what children learn from their parents about the value of living a Jewish life is a far more penetrating lesson than anything they will learn outside the home.

Many Jewish teens stop their formal Jewish education after they become bar or bat mitzvah at about age thirteen. In no other area of serious endeavor would we say that the educational level attained by age thirteen is sufficient for optimum functioning, yet many Jewish parents somehow accept this minimal education as adequate for their children.

Jewish identity studies released during the past five years or so have demonstrated the strong positive correlation between Jewish affiliation in adulthood and participation during the teen years in Jewish formal and informal educational activities, such as youth groups, high school programs, summer camps, trips to Israel, and social action initiatives. Parental influence, these studies indicate, is a significant factor in the teens' decision to join and to stay connected.[4]

Shortly before her bat mitzvah, our eldest daughter informed me that she planned to stop going to Hebrew school after the bat mitzvah celebration. "Jenny," I said (she was still Jenny back then), "you know that our family is committed to lifelong Jewish learning." What this actually meant at that point in time was that my husband and I, who hadn't ourselves received a Jewish education as children, were still trying to catch up to our kids' level of learning.

"I know, Mom," she replied, "but no one else in my class comes after their bar or bat mitzvah. I'll be the only one." She was telling the truth, I knew, and I was in a bad spot. Uncertain as to how to proceed, I said, "Dad and I expect you to go to a Hebrew high school program." A long silence ensued during which I mostly prayed. Getting no answer, I decided that if she still objected, I would drop it. "Okay," she said, "I'll think about it." When I asked her recently what recommendations she would have for parents of Jewish teens today, this is what she said in her e-mail: "Investigate the option of Hebrew high school with your child. Not only will it continue their Jewish education, but they may form lifetime Jewish friendships."

Developing "Yours, Mine, and Ours" Strategies

In my opinion, the most important thing to remember about Jewish observance as you move through the transition of your child's teenage years is that you may want to strike a balance between your view of what Jewish life should be and your teenager's own reality. Beyond that, you want to have a relationship that will endure after the teenage years have passed. How can you accomplish this? Here are some suggestions:

- Pick the essential principles that you can't compromise on and be flexible on the rest. This only works, of course, if you don't have a zillion nonnegotiable principles! The teenage years are definitely the time to choose your battles carefully in terms of

Jewish observance. I know families from every stream of Judaism who expect their teens to be home for parts of Shabbat and who turn a blind eye to where their kids are the rest of that time.

- If necessary, enable your child to live a different "Shabbat reality" in your observant home. I've known observant parents whose teens listened to music, spoke on the phone, and watched television in their bedroom with the door closed. In our home, since we didn't have TVs and computers in the bedrooms, we put a TV and a VCR in the basement where our teens and their friends could gather as my husband and I lived in an electronics-free Shabbat world upstairs. For this bifurcated Shabbat fiction to work, however, both sides have to be respectful of each other's presence and behave accordingly.

- Acknowledge that when your child is a teenager, he or she may prefer to have sleepovers at a less-observant friend's home than at yours. There, he or she will most likely engage in activities not available at home. We found it interesting and affirming, though, how much our teens' friends—Jewish and non-Jewish alike—enjoyed sharing the beauty of our Friday-evening Sabbath dinner with us.

- Accept the fact that as your teens hit the later teenage years and go off to college, their comings and goings may not always coincide exactly with your preferences for arrivals and departures in terms of the Sabbath and the holidays. I personally found this very difficult, but my husband and I chose to let them come and go as they wished because we thought their presence was a greater value than their absence would be if we placed upon them restrictions they couldn't or wouldn't respect.

- Encourage or persuade them to go to shul with you when they are home for the Jewish holidays, no matter how much they might initially protest. The community deserves the joy of seeing that beautiful young Jewish adult who grew up before their eyes!

- Try to find news ways of participating in Jewish life together. For some families, this might mean becoming active in social action projects, like volunteering at a homeless shelter. For others, it might be the creation of new family rituals, like celebrating the completion of a school semester or the end of a sports season in which the teen participated. Some possibilities for creating new rituals can be found at the myjewishlearning website: www.myjewishlearning.com/xcommon/HowToGuides.htm.

Our children are the next link in the tradition that goes back to Mount Sinai. At some point, their vision will define what Judaism will be in their generation. Our ability to share our views and our perspectives with one another will help us both, as we turn the future over to them and as they assume leadership with confidence. Our job is to keep them engaged, even as we model the kind of Jewish behavior and values we wish to transmit to future generations.

When I asked my children what advice should be given to parents of Jewish teens today, our now married twenty-six-year-old daughter responded: "Let your Jewish teens know that no matter what, you will always love them." One way we can show our love for our children is to give them the tools they will need to live a life that is rich in meaning and purpose, despite the challenges and the difficulties of any given moment.

7

From Control to Consultation

In Chapter 2, we considered the often painful feelings parents may experience as their teenagers pull away in order to grow into healthy adulthood. For Jewish parents in particular, especially for those who have lived the joys and laughter of dreidels spinning wildly, matzah sandwiches crumbling, and little faces in the glow of Sabbath and holiday candles, the onset of the teenager years can feel like the end of life's most wonderful chapter. What, we might ask, lies beyond?

In the Parenting Jewish Teens workshops I lead at synagogues, Jewish community centers, and professional conferences, I ask participants to share with the group words or phrases that describe some aspect of their relationship with their children when the children were little. Here are some of the responses I typically hear:

"Dependence"

"They thought I was all-knowing."

"Security"

"Physical closeness"

"She respected me."

"Control"

"Hugs and kisses"

You can add to this list any that come to mind about your own relationship with your child when he or she was little. I then ask participants to describe in words or phrases their vision for the relationship between them and their children when their children (now teens) become adults; in other words, what are they hoping for? These are the kind of responses I often hear:

"Closeness"

"Mutual respect"

"Independence" (some say "interdependence")

"Shared Jewish values and lifestyle"

"Hugs"

"Friendship/companionship"

There is occasionally disagreement and discussion around this last point. Some parents express discomfort with the idea of children as friends, and this is appropriate, especially when children are teenagers, as we noted in Chapter 5 (Family Relationships). Since I always put this item on the list if no one else does, let me clarify and defend it: a parent and a child can never be equals, as we might mean in the usual sense of the word *friend* as in "buddy." As Jews, we should not cross the boundary of the fifth commandment: "Honor your father and your mother." We can, however, experience friendship with our young adult/adult children in another way. It can include all the characteristics on the wish list, and the relationship that emerges can transcend any of the wonderful feelings we experienced in our parenting before they entered adolescence. Believe me, it is worth working toward.

At this point, we have on one side the relationship with our children when they were little and on the other side a vision for the relationship when they are grown. So what is in the middle? Exactly! The teenage years. The question is, how do we get from here to there? How do we redesign our relationship with our teenage children in such a way as to achieve the outcome that will be best for them and for us? A visual representation of this question appears in the diagram "The Jewish Parenting Continuum." Although it may seem easier to focus on the changes in behavior that we want from our teens, the truth is that for our teens to change, *we as parents must change first.* Put another way, for our children to make the transition through the teenage years to healthy, happy adulthood with family relationships relatively intact, parents must change so that their kids can grow. This is not an easy thing to do, as we saw in Chapter 2, where hurt parental feelings can stand in the way of mature judgment and helpful facilitation. Dr. Linda Sonna, author of *The Everything Parenting a Teenager Book: A Survival Guide for Parents!* puts it this way:

> While much is made of teen mood swings and unpredictable behavior, many parents find themselves feeling and acting like adolescents themselves. They overreact to small problems, explode over minor difficulties and become hypercritical nags. The stress of dealing with a young know-it-all can certainly explain these bouts of emotionality and losses of temper, but often there is more to it than that. It is common for parents to go through a midlife crisis just as their child is preparing in earnest to leave home."[1]

The Jewish Parenting Continuum

CHILDHOOD	TEEN YEARS	ADULTHOOD
When our children are young, the relationship is characterized by:		When our children are adults, we would like the relationship to be characterized by:

- Dependence
- Control
- Respect for parental authority
- Physical contact, closeness

- Independence/ Interdependence
- Respect for family (Jewish) values
- Mutual respect and acceptance
- Companionship

How does *our* behavior have to change during the teen years
to help our children get from here to there?

Noted therapist Dr. Robert Brooks writes and speaks extensively about the concept of "resilience"—the capacity to grow and adjust to life's changing circumstances in a positive and constructive way. I would suggest that in the struggles large and small for power and control in our relationships with our teens, the following words have much to say to parents about taking the first steps toward peaceful change:

> If we are seeking our happiness by hoping that someone else changes first, then we will have a difficult time initiating the necessary steps to change. However, if we entertain the belief that change, even in small quantities, is within our grasp and that we are the authors of our own lives, we are more likely to pursue new behaviors. In turn, if these new behaviors lead to a more productive, satisfying lifestyle, they will reinforce a more optimistic mind-set, resulting in further positive changes in our behavior.[2]

What can Jewish parents do to help their teenager through the separation/maturation process?

1. Acknowledge your feelings. This may be easier said than done, especially if your relationship with your child was loving and close when he or she was younger. It's okay to feel hurt and rejection when your teenager hurts and seems to reject you; however, being aware of your feelings doesn't mean you have to act on them. On the contrary, being aware of difficult feelings enables you to refrain from reacting inappropriately, and enables you to behave as a responsible parent in the face of provocation, rather than as a vindictive child. There is a serious, life-altering shift going on here, and the more in touch you can be with your deeper feelings, the better able you will be to address the situation in a productive way.

2. Transfer decision making, wherever possible. For younger teens, this may be as limited as involving them in a conversation about the decision and taking their feelings and preferences seriously.

For older teens, this may mean actually letting them make decisions with which you strongly disagree, as long as those decisions don't jeopardize health and safety. For example, as scary as it was to us, my husband and I allowed our then sixteen-year-old son to organize and run a teen club night in Manhattan (what were we thinking?). On the other hand, even when our teens were off at college, where parents are treated by the administration as aliens with no rights whatsoever except to pay bills, we intervened with the administration when we determined that health and safety issues were at stake. Of course, our kids hated us for this, but this is not a popularity contest—and amazingly few parents ever really get fired from this job for doing the right thing.

3. Whenever possible, opt for the role of transportation provider before your teen starts driving. "Car time" conversations can have a unique quality, and teens sometimes open up and speak in ways they otherwise won't. A friend of ours recalls the meaningful, adultlike conversations he was able to have with his daughter before she left for college. "It was a parent's dream," he chuckles. "She couldn't walk out on me, even if I inadvertently said something that pissed her off." If you live in a city like New York, where teens can make their way around without your help, you'll have to find an alternative, such as regular Sunday-morning brunches, weekday-evening dessert at a favorite place, or the like. This is especially important when they are high school seniors, and the excitement and the tension of the imminent departure from home if they are going off to college can have a really wacky effect on all concerned.

4. Work toward accepting your child for who he or she is, or is becoming, instead of holding on to old dreams, hopes, and expectations. The concept of parents as loving custodians for their children who ultimately "belong" to God appears in various places in Jewish writings and is beautifully expressed here by a Christian minister, Thomas C. Short:

> All husbands and wives borrow their children. Our children are not our own; our children belong to God.... They are not ours to keep, but to rear. They are not given to us to mold into our image. They are not given to us so that we can force them to fulfill our lives and thus, in some way, cancel our failures. They are not tools to be used, but souls to be loved.[3]

This idea of dreams and expectations will be explored again in Chapter 9.

5. Let them fail, if need be. In point #2 above, I mentioned our son's teen club night event in Manhattan, which was a fabulous social success and an abysmal financial failure. The problem was that no one had actually secured a contract for the planned, larger venue, and a last-minute change to a smaller, unpublicized venue became necessary, which negatively impacted revenues. Even though his agreement with his investors was a share in the earnings but no liability for him if there were losses, my husband and I felt that he should return the money his friends had invested and lost because we were concerned about his reputation in the community. This decision cost him his personal savings account, plus earnings for the next eighteen months. After some of the pain had subsided, I asked him what lesson he had learned from this experience. "Next time," he said, "I'll be sure to have a lawyer check the contract." Did I mention that his father and I had cautioned him to do just that before any money changed hands?

6. Consider psychotherapy. In a world characterized by frenzied lifestyles, micro-nuclear families, and the absence of supportive communities, therapy can be a powerful aid in working through the challenges of this often difficult time of life. Although the inclination is often to rush our kids into the therapist's office when things get bumpy, teen behavior is not necessarily a separate, isolated "problem." For this reason, therapy for parents or family therapy can be important as well. I can't help but be reminded of the model of the four children at the

Passover seder: is the *rasha,* that wicked child, ever going to change? Probably not, if we keep talking to him in the same rejecting way.

7. Form Jewish parenting support groups. Remember the beginning of Chapter 3 where I described the warmth and sense of shared values and community that permeated my father's (Old Country) family? Most of us don't have that today, nor do we have the kind of parenting groups like Mommy and Me classes at the synagogue or JCC that were so helpful when our children were little. The parents of Jewish teens need assistance in making the transition from control to consultation. We need to talk, share, and learn from one another on this journey.

Here's an example of what I mean. A while ago, a dear friend approached me to thank me for the Parenting Jewish Teens workshop he had attended when his son was in high school. He reported that at the workshop, he had shared with the group his intense frustration about what he saw as his son's complete indifference about grades and about the college application process. I, who already had two in college, apparently had asked: "Do you think that Josh [name disguised] will graduate from high school?" "Of course he will," my friend had replied. "Do you think he'll want to stay home and get a job, or do you think he'll want to go off to college?" I asked. He thought about that for a minute and responded, "I think he'll want to go to college." "Then," I replied, "the question isn't whether Josh will go to college. The question is, which college will Josh go to? And isn't that really his decision to make, given that his choice fits your family's financial constraints?" It was as if my friend had been struck by a thunderbolt. "You're right!" he exclaimed. "This isn't my problem!" The sequel: Josh went to college, he has done just fine, and his dad thinks I'm a genius. No, I'm just someone who could help him work through his concern, parent to parent. We have to be able to do this for one another. And we may need to advocate for ways we can do this within the Jewish places whose mission it is to support Jewish family life.

Tsimtsum

The complex notion of *tsimtsum* is a fascinating concept in Jewish thought. It refers to the mystical notion that God's presence once filled all of creation. God then withdrew, or contracted, to make room for human freedom and choice. In this contracting, God made space for independent human endeavor—and responsibility.

This is a fascinating model for the parents of Jewish teens. As parents, we need to engage in *tsimtsum,* to pull back in order to provide our teenage children with the space in which they can grow. This is not about abandonment or indifference! Engaging in *tsimtsum* in this way is about stepping back with love and caring concern to facilitate the transition from childhood to healthy young adulthood. As Rabbi Bradley Shavit Artson of the University of Judaism, writes:

> While casting a giant shadow over our children's perceptions and actions, their maturation entails a retreat of the parents' ability to impose their own preferences. Ultimately, children learn to become responsible for themselves and their own behavior. Can we, as parents, learn to let our children take charge?[4]

Holiday Homecoming

Sometimes, even after you think you've gotten there, you find out that you really haven't.

I don't know why holiday homecomings were as difficult as they were. No matter what the level of teenage rebellion or discontent had been like in the earlier period, the first freshman-year holiday visit home was fraught with conflict. They *had* come home—I suppose that is something—and they came to synagogue with us, also no small thing. But before the brief holiday was over, each one of my children picked a fight in his or her own way, destroying the moment and leaving me mystified and profoundly sad. On the first evening of Rosh Hashanah, for example, one of them even got up from the holiday table during dinner for no reason that was apparent to my husband or to me, jumped into the car, and drove back to school that very night. What in the world was going on?

The holiday visit home from college marks a new level of separation, I think, as the teenager/young adult struggles to define him- or herself in a way that is truly separate from membership in the family of origin, with all its policies, practices, and rules. This human being is now a person we only partly know, and that is the part we want to hold close and celebrate with as we always have. But the rest of that human being is becoming a new person who wants to define the world on his or her own terms—including the way core experiences like Jewish holiday observances will be lived. Intellectually, I know this is a good thing and if I believe in all that came before—when she was little and rushed to put the challah on the table, and he was small and loved to fold the napkins—then I must believe that someday they will create their own homes filled with ritual and meaning, homes that will be different than ours has been, but ones that I will recognize just the same. This is the hope, of course. Still, it's so hard to watch them go—and maybe knowing that I feel the way I do makes them need to break away even more.

Even so, *hineini*. I'll be here the next time they are ready to land.

8

Interdating and Intermarriage

It is difficult to have an unemotional conversation about intermarriage in America today in almost any setting. Few Jewish parents are indifferent to the religious affiliation of their child's choice of life partner, while Jewish communal professionals and lay leaders are, for the most part, working hard to shore up our children's Jewish identity to avert the possibility of their "marrying out" when the time for committed mating arrives. This chapter addresses two important topics related to intermarriage: teen inter-dating and guiding your teen if you are intermarried.

According to studies conducted during the past decade, such as the United Jewish Communities (UJC) 2000–2001 National Jewish Population Survey, intermarriage rates between Jews and non-Jews in America have increased sharply, compared to those of previous generations.[1] One important finding of these studies has been that the chances of self-identifying as Jewish and marrying another Jew are far greater when both parents are Jewish. This is true, though not in equal numbers, whether both parents were born Jewish or whether one was born Jewish and the other converted to Judaism.

Young Jewish adults, however, tend not to see the question of intermarriage in macro-communal terms; they simply fall in love with another human being and choose to spend their life in that relationship. For the most part, they cannot understand what all the fuss is about. Even those who received a solid Jewish education and participated actively in Jewish life do not see marrying a non-Jew as the death knell for their Jewish identity. They have been raised in a free, open society and have not experienced in America the externally imposed boundaries and the anti-Semitism that kept the Jewish people separate and apart in other times and places. The reality is that your child can comfortably intermarry in this country and lead a successful and satisfying life. If he or she chooses, your child can join a synagogue and participate actively, intermarried or not, because the fact of intermarriage doesn't change your child's status as a Jew: born one, he or she will always be one unless he or she converts to another faith.

This situation changes dramatically, however, when children arrive on the scene. Issues regarding the children's religious identity and education, and how to celebrate holidays and life-cycle events can be quite vexing, even with the many resources that are available to intermarried families today. Matters of style and substance continue to be differences that need to be negotiated and resolved, even in homes where conversion to Judaism has occurred. Given all this, can there be any positives in the situation?

Intermarriage Is Nothing New

There are numerous accounts of intermarriage in the Bible. The Egyptian pharaoh gave to Joseph as a wife the daughter of the high priest of Egypt (Gen. 41:45). Moses was married to the daughter of a Midianite priest (Exod. 2:15–22), and his brother Aaron and sister Miriam later spoke out against Moses because of this (Num. 12:1). The Book of Ruth tells the famous story of a non-Jewish (Moabite) woman whose Jewish husband died and who chose to remain with her mother-in-law and to join the Jewish people: "Do not urge me to leave you, to turn back and not follow you. For wherever you go, I will go; wherever you lodge, I will lodge; your people shall be my people, and your God my God" (Ruth 1:11). According to our tradition, King David was a direct descendent of Ruth, and it is believed the Messiah will be a direct descendent of King David.

It seems to me that our response to intermarriage has had much to do with the places and the circumstances in which we have found ourselves. Not surprisingly, when Jews have interacted freely with the larger society, intermarriage has been more likely to occur; when we have been isolated and kept apart, the opposite has been true. The boundaries between Jews and non-Jews in America are virtually nonexistent, and we therefore see rates of intermarriage that can be causes for concern in terms of Jewish continuity. These rates are unlikely to change, in my opinion, unless there is a dramatic and most unwelcome change in the circumstances of Jews within the larger American society.

On the other hand, I have heard some Jewish communal leaders express the sentiment that intermarriage is not necessarily a bad thing for a people whose numbers have been unnaturally reduced by persecutions like the Holocaust. Perhaps, as the argument goes, we might see intermarriage as an opportunity to "gain another Jew" rather than simply wring our hands about the loss of one to intermarriage. Much depends upon how we address the situation. Organizations like the Jewish Outreach Institute, for example, are dedicated to empowering and helping the Jewish community "welcome and fully embrace all members of interfaith families into Jewish life," according to the mission statement posted on their website (www.joi.org).

What if, however, you are intermarried? How does the situation change? Let's take a look.

For Parents Who Intermarried

Parenting children in an interfaith marriage is not easy. I should know; I did it. At the outset, my husband and I had decided that one religion in the home would be best for our children and we had agreed that the religion would be Judaism. Of course, at the time, neither of us had a clue as to what that really entailed. Although my husband eventually converted to Judaism, we still had to address many of the issues faced by interfaith couples for whom Jewish identity or affiliation is important, including how to handle holidays (his family's) and life-cycle events (our family's).

Parents who did not choose one religion for their home or who chose no religion for their home may find their teenagers searching for this additional dimension of their identity. According to the outreach professionals with whom I have spoken, it is not uncommon for teens in this situation to feel anger at their parents for having abdicated their responsibility for this important decision, leaving it to the child to decide. At a time when teens tend to ask the big existential life questions that religions provide a framework for addressing, teens who have not been given a religious identity and a corresponding education can feel the absence of a language with which to have this conversation. They can also feel significant conflict at this time because making a commitment about their own identity may seem, at some level, like choosing between their parents. "Issues that may have been swept under the carpet before because they were considered too hard to deal with now come out in full force," observes Kathy Kahn, director of Outreach and Synagogue Community for the Union for Reform Judaism. The best thing parents can do in this situation is to be open and honest in their communications with their teens, advise Kahn and Rabbi Kerry Olitzky of the Jewish Outreach Institute. They suggest that parents have the conversations with their children now, even though they weren't able to do this when the children were younger.

"Don't be reactive to the anger your teen may express," advises Jo Kay, director of the New York School of Education of Hebrew Union College–Jewish Institute of Religion. "Empathize rather than argue, and help your teen work through these difficult issues. It's an opportunity for you to enter a dialogue that will strengthen your child and, if handled properly, can engender feelings of mutual respect." Be candid about why you made the decisions you did, and acknowledge the truth of your children's reality in terms of the unexpected impact your decision may have had on them.

Teens raised as Jews may want to know more about the non-Jewish parent's religion at this time. While encouraging this exploration, both parents may want to take this opportunity to explain (or revisit) the decision you made to raise your children as Jews. You may find yourself challenged to explain your own Jewish identity and beliefs, and this may be a good time for you to engage in further study as a Jewish adult, both on an individual basis and together as a family. If you want Jewish outcomes for your teens, it is important to encourage their involvement in the formal and informal Jewish education programs mentioned later in this chapter. You may also want to consult the resources listed in the "Interfaith Families" section of Appendix A.

Up Close and Personal

Years after I was married and the mother of three, my father, of blessed memory, asked me a startling question. "What would have happened," he wanted to know, "if Ron hadn't gone along with all this? What if he hadn't converted to Judaism and been willing to get involved in Jewish family life the way you decided you wanted to?" My dad loved Ron like a son, so this question was a serious one and deserved a serious reply. I thought about it for a while and replied, "I guess we would have gotten divorced."

Somewhere I remember coming across some statistics that indicated a higher rate of divorce among intermarried couples than among the general population. I can't remember the source, but I certainly can identify with the finding. Being intermarried and trying to raise Jewish children is often complicated and conflicting. Even when your spouse converts to Judaism, as mine did, the problems may change and even ease somewhat, but they do not go away. Sometimes you can't even tell if the causes of tension between the two of you are normal husband-and-wife interactions, your own particular personality differences, or the subtle religious identity and related cultural differences that always seem to lurk beneath the surface.

Of course, it will never be possible to know the total impact that religious and cultural differences between the parents have on their children. Ron describes how this problem became real to him in a way it never had before when Jenny, our firstborn, was only three years old:

"When I came home from work one day, Joanne told me that Jenny had asked her why Daddy is different. When asked what she meant by 'different,' Jenny had said, 'Daddy isn't Jewish like the rest of our family.'

"The implications of Jen's question floored me. My first reaction was that I didn't want to be different than the rest of my family, though it would be several more years before I removed that difference by converting to Judaism. The larger insight that came from Jenny's question, though, was how important the sense of a unified family identity was to her. Experiencing Christmas with my side of the family and Jewish holidays with Joanne's must have been confusing to her. The need for a single identity in our home that could serve as an anchor through our children's formative years and beyond became the motivating factor that moved me toward the conversion my wife had never requested."

As our children entered the dating years, both Ron and I spoke with them as frankly as we could about the desirability of finding a life partner of their same religious faith. This has been an extremely difficult and sensitive conversation, since their father is quite naturally a model for them and since they are blessed to have non-Jewish relatives whom they love dearly. In addition, the disparity between what we say and what we ourselves did has no doubt made their own decision-making more difficult. Each of our children is a strongly identified Jewish adult and we hope that they will ultimately establish Jewish homes in which to raise their children, no matter who their choice of marriage partner may be. Even so, Ron and I realize that our children cannot possibly understand how difficult putting our Jewish family life together has been, and how much we would hope that their lives will be easier than ours.

What You Can Do

If you would like to guide your teenager toward eventually choosing a Jewish life partner, here are some suggestions to consider:

- First, acknowledge what you can control and what you can't, and invest your energy in the former. You can't, for example, control who your kid sits next to, and possibly falls in love with, in algebra class, so don't waste time worrying about that. Instead, pay attention to the three factors that have been identified as positively correlated to Jewish in-marriage in a recent study by Professor Sylvia Barack Fishman: (1) intensive Jewish education, formal and informal, that continues into the teenage years (such as summer camp, youth groups, Israel trips, Hebrew high school), (2) an actively Jewish home in which Judaism is a lived experience, and (3) Jewish friendship circles.[2] The take-away from this is clear: if you want to increase the likelihood that your teen will marry another Jew, maintain or increase your own Jewish home life and be firm about your teen's continued involvement with Jewish activities.

- Encourage your children to envision what they would like their home/family to be like years in the future, when they are married and have a family of their own. Guide your teens through the conversation about how difficult or easy that vision will be to implement with a Jewish or a non-Jewish partner, and facilitate their thought process so that they can reach appropriate conclusions. You can do this even if you chose a spouse who was not born or raised a Jew; sharing your own difficulties (without, of course, unwittingly criticizing your partner) may help your teens bring these issues into sharper focus.

- Expose the "we're only dating" myth. Ellyn Geller, a very special friend and former colleague who made aliyah (return to Israel) upon her retirement from her position as a regional outreach director for the Union of American Hebrew Congregations (now Union for Reform Judaism), developed a workshop for Jewish teens called But Mom, We're Just Dating…. She questioned the kids who said they wanted to marry Jews but would date non-Jews they didn't intend to marry: "So what message are you sending these non-Jewish boyfriends and girlfriends? Are you saying they are good enough to date, but not good enough to marry? Wouldn't it be more respectful simply to say that since you intend to marry someone who is Jewish, you've decided that it would be best to date only Jews, though you are happy to have non-Jews as close, non-romantic friends?" She also made the cogent point that though we have control over whom we choose to date, we don't have control over feelings of love that may develop in a dating relationship. Ellyn led sessions like these at Jewish summer camps and at youth group meetings—yet another indication of the value of teen involvement in Jewish-community-sponsored programs.

Ultimately, it is important to remember that your teen's or young adult's choices might be different from what you would have wished, but they don't necessarily represent a rejection of you and your values. Our job is to give our children the tools, and hopefully the motivation, they need to make Jewish choices, but we ultimately have no control over the outcome. The *v'ahavta* blessing that follows the Shema in the synagogue prayer service cites the commandment from the Book of Deuteronomy to teach our children Torah, and, by implication, how to live a Jewish life. We need to focus on doing that to the best of our ability, at every age and stage of the life cycle. Ultimately, that is the extent of our responsibility and our control. We can, however, resolve to be there to encourage our children's intention to create a Jewish home and to support their raising *their* children as Jews, no matter who their choice of marriage partner may be. As we learn from *Pirkei Avot (The Ethics of the Ancestors),* we are not obligated to complete the task, though neither are we released from the responsibility of trying (2:21).

9

Conclusion:
The Blessing of Teens

It never ceases to amaze me how our teenagers can strike at the very heart of things, often when we are least prepared to respond. In one of those difficult theological debates that teens seem to love having, my mostly grown son asked: "Mom, what does it really matter if we believe in God or not? What difference does it actually make if we believe that God exists, or if we don't?"

I had never really thought about the matter quite that way before, but I'm a big believer in answering the tough ones, so I pondered the question for some time. Finally, I answered: "To live without a sense of God in your life is to live without a sense of blessing. To live without a sense of blessing is to simply exist, to put one foot in front of the other every minute of every day. Some may call this 'life,'" I concluded, "but I can't see how that is a life much worth living." What I have come to know since then is that the power of blessing is often in our very own hands.

In this final chapter, we will discover how three traditional Jewish concepts can reveal the blessing of parenting Jewish teens today.

Berachah—Blessing

It is a traditional and quite beautiful practice for Jewish parents to bless their children after welcoming the Sabbath into the home on

Friday night. An ancient formulaic blessing is recited, to which we will soon turn our attention. But first, I have a confession to make. Friday nights in our home when our children were teenagers was often far from idyllic. Despite the best of intentions, real life often intruded, as the tensions and the difficulties of normal parent-teen relationships found their way into what should otherwise have been a joyous and peaceful time. Nevertheless, we never gave up, and every Friday night found us at the Shabbat table once again. Where we still are, which is quite a blessing in itself.

The practice of parents blessing their children on Shabbat has its origin in the Torah. When the patriarch Jacob lay on his deathbed, his son Joseph visited him, bringing along his own sons (Jacob's grandsons). Noticing them, Jacob asked that they come closer so that he could bless them. It is this blessing, the one that Jacob gave to his two grandsons, Ephraim and Menasseh, that Jewish parents use to this very day to bless our own sons every time we welcome the Sabbath or a Jewish holiday into our homes: "May God make you like Ephraim and Menasseh" (Gen. 48:20). But who, we might ask, were Ephraim and Manessah, and why would we want our sons to be like them?

Well, the first thing is, they weren't Jewish, at least by today's standards. Their father Joseph was born and raised a Jew, of course, but after being sold as a slave by his brothers and rising to a position of great prominence in Egypt, he had been given the Egyptian name Zaphenath-paneah by the pharaoh, who also gave him the daughter of an Egyptian priest as a wife. Only the most fanciful rabbinic midrashim (stories or legends) could rewrite this text to make these boys Jewish—a non-Jewish mother, a completely assimilated father … not much to work with here. So why would we want to bless our sons with the hope that they grow to be like Ephraim and Menasseh?

I think the answer lies in the grandparent's heart. Jacob saw, or chose to be blind to, the reality of the grandsons who stood before him. The situation was what it was, and no amount of hand-wringing or self-recrimination could change the past: Joseph had been lost to his father for many years, probably as a result of Jacob's own flagrant favoritism and the hostility it engendered in Joseph's siblings. Under the circumstances, Joseph had made the best life that he could. Far away from family and community, he had crafted his life with a new family and a new community, and here were his sons, the products of his changed circumstance. Perhaps Jacob understood all that, but in looking at his grandsons, he saw beyond the moment, as grandparents often do. Jacob's blessing was not so much an affirmation of what he saw, I believe, but was rather an expression of hope for what might yet be: not Jewish today, but maybe Jewish tomorrow, not leaders of our people today, but maybe leaders tomorrow.

Later in our people's history, twelve tribes of Israel emerged. Among them were the tribes of Ephraim and Menasseh.

Here is my takeaway from this story: It can often seem as though we are battling with our teenage children on a minute-to-minute basis. As they are growing into who they will become, they assert their right to be less—or just different—than our dreams of them. We fell in love with them when they were so small, so irresistibly precious and innocent. And we fell in love with our dreams of who they would someday be. As they struggle to make sense of their lives in a world they had no hand in creating, we see their flaws and their failures that can be so hard for us to accept. And we struggle to find the often elusive sense of equilibrium that will enable us to love and accept them with their emerging pimples and blemishes, outside and in. What we need to do, in the end, is what Jacob did: embrace the children who stand before us just as they are, and bless them with the vision of a future we may or may not live to see.

Teshuvah—Repentance

Our lives are like an intricate web, woven with threads of the past into the present. As William Faulkner observed, "Not only is the past relevant, it's not even done!"[1] Looking back on the parent I was when my children were teenagers often fills me with regret: if I had only been better, smarter, more present, less distracted. If only I'd had the benefit of nurturing parenting myself. If only my marriage had been easier. If only I had insisted on additional opinions when I sensed something was wrong, but nothing really showed. If only, if only, if only …

It's easy to get lost in feelings like these when thinking about how our own frailties and failures affected our children. But on the High Holy Days, and every time we participate in a weekday prayer service, we get the message loud and clear that although we can't change the past, we have the power to bring healing, to repair the present, and to change the future.

The root of the Hebrew word for repentance *(teshuvah)* means "to turn" or "to return." This is about more than receiving God's forgiveness for the things we may have knowingly or inadvertently done wrong—it's about taking responsibility for doing the often excruciating difficult work of assessing ourselves and correcting the patterns, habits, and behaviors that need to change. As Rabbi Arthur Green explains:

> One of the most important and original terms of Jewish moral thought, *teshuvah,* is quite inadequately rendered by the usual translation "repentance." To repent is to turn away from sin and seek forgiveness. *Teshuvah* is a broader concept, one that goes to the very root of human existence…. Human life is inconceivable without *teshuvah.*[2]

Each of us has the opportunity to forge our own unique way to the introspection and change that will enable us to become more reflective, more deeply sensitive, and more constructive parents, no matter how old we are, and no matter how old our children may be. For me, the need to change came during my eldest daughter's senior year of high school. It was triggered by something that happened while I was attending a teacher-training workshop at a colleague's synagogue one day. During the lunch break, her seventeen-year-old daughter came joyfully bounding into the room. She consulted with her mother briefly and left. I asked my colleague whether her daughter didn't have school that day and she replied, "Yes, but I let her take the day off. She wants to major in film in college and Julia

Roberts is in town shooting a movie, so I arranged to get permission for my daughter to be on the set." "It's okay with you that she misses a day of school in the first semester of her senior year?" I asked incredulously. "Of course," my colleague replied. "I trust her to get her work done, but more than that, I want her to still like me enough to want to have lunch with me when she and I get older."

It was in that moment that I realized I had been more of a problem for my teenagers than they had been for me. I realized that if I wanted our lives to be different, I would have to be like the Israelite, Nachshon ben Aminadav, who, according to rabbinic legend, was the first to step into the Reed Sea as the Israelites were helplessly trapped by water on one side and by Pharaoh's pursuing army on the other. As the story goes, Nachshon took the risk of entering the waters while everyone else stood panicked and helpless. When he was in so deep that the sea reached his nostrils, God parted the waters for the Israelites so they could pass through in safety to the freedom that awaited them on the other side (BT, *Sotah* 37a).

The message seems pretty clear to me: if we want things to change, we need to be willing to take the risk ourselves, with no assurance as to what the outcome will be. That is the message of *teshuvah,* and that is the key to strengthening our family relationships. The good news is that it's never too late for us to do this, and we don't have to do it alone.

Since the beginning of my Jewish journey as an adult, I've been fascinated by the High Holy Days service and by the litany of sins[3] that request forgiveness for the wrongs we have committed. These, rather amazingly, are recited in the plural; that is, it's not me as an individual who is asking for forgiveness, but rather "we" as a community are making the request:

> For the sin we have committed against You by malicious gossip,
> For the sin we have committed against You by our hypocrisy,
> For the sin we have committed before You by disrespect to parents or teachers,
> For the sin we have committed before You by committing bribery ...

What is the sense of this, I have wondered. How can everyone be acknowledging what I personally have done wrong? And why in the world should I be asking forgiveness for other things on that list that I never did?

As we move through the list of transgressions, I find myself saying things like, "Nope, not that one. Not that one either—thank God! Whoops, yup, this next one is definitely me," and so on. But the second time we go through the list, something changes. I sense that this is not just about me personally; this is also about the people standing near me, and about all the people in that particular place at that time, and ultimately about all the Jews who are praying in synagogues around the world that day. Each of us has our own private issues and failings, and possibly demons, which may be too hard to bear alone. So we stand together, and in the sanctuary of that community that surrounds us, we acknowledge to ourselves, and to God, those things that still need our attention. In that experience, the power of "we" is indisputably greater than the power of "me."

> Standing on the parted shores of history
> we still believe what we were taught
> before ever we stood at Sinai's foot;
>
> that wherever we go, it is eternally Egypt
> that there is a better place, a promised land;
> that the winding way to that promise passes through the
>   wilderness
>
> that there is no way to get from here to there
> except by joining hands, marching
> together.[4]

Tikkun—Repair

The term *tikkun olam,* "repair of the world," has come to be associated with actions that improve the world and help make it a better place. The idea of *tikkun olam* is based on a Jewish mystical view of creation, in which vessels containing sparks of God's light were shattered, scattering the sparks throughout the world. The shattered vessels represent a state of brokenness, and as we work to repair that brokenness here on earth, a corresponding repair occurs in the heavenly realm. I think parents can learn a lot about parenting Jewish teens from this idea.[5]

A story is told about a Hasid who wanted to repair the world. He found that it was too big a job, so he decided that he would just change his community instead. That, too, turned out to be more than he could accomplish, so he resolved to fix just his family. Finally, he realized that he did not have the power to do that either, so he concluded that he would have to begin by repairing himself.[6]

The idea of making the world a better place is a beautiful and noble one, and it is through the efforts of so many good people working on so many important causes that life is better for so many of us. As Jews, we call this holy work because it is our way—some would say our responsibility—of being God's partner in the ongoing work of creation.

But perhaps there is a parallel process going on in Jewish family life. Perhaps the relationship between parents and children, especially teenage children, provides the stage on which the work of *tikkun* is played. What if it is true that the struggles in which we engage with our teenage children *are actually meant to be,* not only because our teens are going through a natural stage of separation, but also because their struggles force us to confront the world, not as we knew it or as we wish it to be, but as it actually is. In doing so, we can sometimes glimpse a power greater than ourselves at work.

A tremendous fight took place between our two daughters when they were teenagers. The younger one, then in high school, refused to stay in our home with the older one, then in college, when my husband and I had to be out of town for a wedding. The youngest child, our son, wisely stayed out of the fray. Our younger daughter claimed that her older sister was too bossy, and the older sister claimed she had to be that way because her younger sister was a master at covertly breaking all the rules, but this was not going to happen on her watch. It was clear to me that this fight represented a lot more than the issue that was on the table. I stood in the kitchen with these two hostile protagonists and desperately prayed for a resolution I simply could not see. (I have noticed that my deepest, most heartfelt, and spontaneous prayers—the Hebrew word for this intense feeling is *kavannah*—burst forth around the issues of family in my life.)

I sat down and told my daughters that no one was leaving the table until we had reached a solution to this problem. As you can imagine, there was pushback and (dare I say?) whining, but I remained adamant. We were prisoners of our problem. For what seemed like an eternity, no one spoke. Then, slowly, tentatively and painfully, words emerged. At first, they wouldn't look at one another; instead they directed their words to me, or off into space, but eventually, they confronted each other. During this process, I remained silent. In the end, an agreement was fashioned and they finally turned to me. I said five words: "God was in this place."

If we Jews say that God works in our world, maybe it is the case that our teenagers play a role in our lives that we haven't yet acknowledged. Perhaps there is a reason for the conflict, as they challenge us out of our complacency, forcing us to seek new answers to questions we weren't asking. The very struggle with our teens can keep us younger, sharper, more engaged, as old rules and attitudes are subjected to rigorous—if not exhausting!—debate. And when, after all rational explanations have failed, we find ourselves resorting to the eternal "Do this because I said so and I'm your parent!" are we not perhaps reconnecting in some way to that ultimate limit, the Torah, that keeps us grounded and balanced ("Honor thy father and thy mother")?

In other words, it's not just a matter of surviving our children's teenage years—teenagers can actually teach us something about how we must change and grow as we reach toward holiness and wholeness in our own lives. They make us better than we are. They teach us that arrogance doesn't work. They remove our pretensions and our foolish pride, and they expose us for who we really are:

simply humans, flawed and vulnerable, with the blessed capacity to feel hurt, rejection, and embarrassment. But most of all, our teenagers help us realize that we have the ability to transform a love that was based on our own needs and dreams of perfection into a love that truly cherishes and accepts the other, exactly as he or she is. This is the process of *tikkun*—repair—in our own lives, and our teenagers can make it happen if we are willing to engage.

Hazak, Hazak, V'nithazek—Be Strong, Be Strong, and Let Us Strengthen One Another

The world of our teenagers can be a scary place. The dangers are real and the pressures are great. In a report mentioned earlier, *Hard-wired to Connect: The New Scientific Case for Authoritative Communities,* their world is described by doctors and youth service professionals in these frightening terms:

> The first part [of the crisis] is the deteriorating mental and behavioral health of U.S. children. We are witnessing high and rising rates of depression, anxiety, attention deficit, conduct disorders, thoughts of suicide, and other serious mental, emotional, and behavioral problems among U.S. children and adolescents.[7]

Thomas Friedman, one of the leading journalists of our time, believes that if we don't prepare our young people for the academic and economic realities of the world they will be inheriting, we will be paving their way to a life with far fewer options than we ourselves have enjoyed. In his fascinating book *The World Is Flat,* he writes:

> Put simply, we need a new generation of parents ready to administer tough love: There comes a time when you've got to put away the Game Boys, turn off the television set, put away the iPod, and get your kids down to work.... I am not suggesting that we militarize education, but I am suggesting that we do more to push our young people to go beyond their comfort

zones, to do things right, and to be ready to suffer some short-run pain for longer gain.[8]

Dr. Mel Levine, who has quite rightly become a national icon for understanding and addressing learning diversity, also speaks about the inability of parents today to prepare their teenagers properly for responsible adulthood. He notes:

> Parents should recognize and overcome their often hidden fear of their children. It is not in the best interest of an adolescent for her parents to cede power to her because she might become very sad or do bad things to herself and the family. Of course kids need to be loved, but to an extent they crave tough love. All kids want parents to set limits as a way of showing their concern for their kids.[9]

So the question is: are we not loving our kids enough, or are we loving them too much? How do we as Jewish parents provide the best environment for our teenagers to foster love and connection on the one hand, while encouraging growth and maturity on the other? The answer, it seems to me, is bigger than any one family can construct. Some would say it takes a village, but I say it takes a Jewish community to raise healthy, successful Jewish teenagers and young adults in the world today.

In the *Hardwired to Connect* report, the concept of authoritative communities was introduced. Such communities are "groups of people who are committed to one another over time and who model and pass on at least part of what it means to be a good person and to live a good life."[10] These are Jewish values, and we need to find a way to actualize them, to make them real in our lives and in the lives of our teenagers.

I am advocating that Jewish parents create parenting Jewish teen groups within the already existing institutions of the synagogue and the Jewish community center. These groups can provide support, information, and encouragement as parents move through the work of rearing their children to adulthood. Appendix C of this book contains the model for such a program; it is one approach, and not the only approach that can work.

But the job is not up to the parents of Jewish teens alone. I believe that the power of the Jewish community needs to be directed to this effort, and that it is both possible and easy to do this. Our synagogues, Jewish community centers, and other places of gathering need to step up and help the parents of Jewish teens reclaim or strengthen Jewish family life. Our institutions must become sanctuaries in the truest sense of the word, as they support parents in their efforts, not with models that may have worked a hundred or fifty years ago, but with approaches and models that will work in our lives today.

Each of us can do part of the parenting Jewish teens job alone. Each of us can strive to be a parent who says—and lives—"*Hineini, I am here for you and always will be.*" But if the parenting is to be truly Jewish, we need our community with us in this holy work.

When we come to the end of reading each book of the Torah, we take a moment to celebrate our accomplishment and to express our determination to grow as individuals, even as we acknowledge the power of living in community. *"Hazak, hazak, v'nithazek,"* we say: "Be strong, be strong, and let us strengthen one another." I say that it is within our Jewish communities that we can strengthen one another and our families. Find one, join one, step inside one—and if need be, create one—and let the power of this eternal tradition bring light and peace to your life.

Appendix A: Special Situations

This Appendix section contains a brief introduction and suggested resources for four special parenting teen situations—special needs, sexual orientation, adoption, and divorce. A list of resources for interfaith families is also included. The material presented here does not represent qualified medical or therapeutic advice, and parents may want to consult with a mental health professional if they feel that this would benefit their family's situation.

Special Needs

We can think of special needs as a continuum along which each one of us has a place, with the "norm" being somewhere in the middle. Everyone on either side is considered to have "special needs," a politically correct term used to include, among other things, disabilities and attention issues; behavioral, physical, and cognitive impairment; and autism. Gifted children are also included in the category of special needs. Although they are not the focus of this section, resources pertaining to gifted children have been included in the resource list that follows this section.

Federal law mandates special education for children with special needs until the age of twenty-one. If your child was diagnosed as having special needs earlier on, you have already learned that one of the most important things you can do in parenting a special needs child is to be an advocate to ensure that your child receives all the services and accommodations to which he or she may be entitled. As Dr. Shana Erenberg, chairman of the Department of Education at Hebrew Theological College, and the special needs consultant for the Union for Reform Judaism, insists: "'No' can never be an answer for a parent of a kid with special needs!"

Parenting a special needs teenager brings new challenges. While the teenage years are typically a time of separation and a journey toward independence, this process will be markedly different for the parent and the special needs teen. Parents who have quite naturally and appropriately been deeply involved in their child's care will need to find ways to shift as much responsibility as possible to the teen. This is especially important in matters of physical self-care for more challenged children. For teens whose disabilities place them toward this end of the spectrum, parents will want to focus their efforts on teaching their teens how to handle the basic life skills they need to acquire to live as independently as possible.

For the many parents whose teens have special needs that include issues of impulsivity (ADD, ADHD, and the like), the normal teenage experimentation with potentially risky behaviors can be alarming and may require closer monitoring. While successful parenting is about helping your child make choices, special needs teens have a harder time making good choices, and parents should be attentive to striking a balance between supervision and autonomy. Candid but sensitive conversations between teens and parents will be helpful in working through these issues. In addition, peer/support groups for both parents and special needs teens can be very useful during this transitional stage.

Parenting a special needs child into Jewish adulthood poses additional and unique challenges. The strong culture of learning and educational achievement that exists within the Jewish community can send an unintended message that there is something "wrong" with the individual who cannot meet the normative standards. "We're all about education—it is the Jewish communal myth, writ large," Rabbi Paula Mack Drill told me. "When you are the parent of a child who is outside the norm, it's as though there is an escalator—it seems as if everyone is going in the same direction, except your child, who doesn't quite fit on the escalator, and he—and you—are left behind."

This problem can be particularly pronounced in formal Jewish educational settings, such as day schools or congregational schools. The special needs child who can hardly make it through the school day has additional hours of schooling beyond that time in both of these formal educational settings. Moreover, while some Jewish day schools do an excellent job of providing services for special needs children and teens, more often such schools lack the financial resources to do so, forcing families to make a painful choice between doing what they believe is best for the child educationally and what they believe is best for the child Jewishly. It is not uncommon for families who find themselves in this situation to experience feelings of abandonment by the Jewish educational system.

Finally, there is the issue of social interactions for special needs teens. In the best of cases, special needs students who have been involved in synagogue-based youth groups are welcomed and well integrated into the group, especially if the special needs child has grown up in a close, supportive synagogue community. Unfortunately, families report that there are many more situations in which the special needs teen feels excluded, as the other teens form small groups or cliques within the youth group, often based on their daytime schooling relationships, which often don't include the special needs child. Parents should be strongly proactive in finding Jewish social settings that will be helpful for their special needs teens. In particular, Jewish summer camps that offer special needs options are a good choice, and there is some information provided below.

Resources

- "Teens with Disabilities—Transition to Adulthood" can be found at *BellaOnline: The Voice of Women,* www.bellaonline. com/articles/art33519.asp.
- "My Son Is Not His Illness," by Rabbi Bradley Shavit Artson. This is a deeply moving account of one father's special love for

his special child. Found on *Sh'ma: An Online Journal of Jewish Responsibility,* www.shma.com/dec99/illness.htm.

- *Spirit* magazine, an online publication for families with special needs children, geared toward the Orthodox community, but is helpful to all Jewish families with special needs children and teens: www.spiritmag.org/.

- The Jewish Education Service of North America (JESNA) provides educational leadership and support services to the federations and other Jewish organizations in North America. You can access valuable information and support materials by going to this location on their website and selecting the links that interest you: www.jesna.org/sosland/kwsearch.asp?kwsearch=special+needs#Websites.

- The Council for Jews with Special Needs is a nonprofit organization that serves Jewish individuals who have special needs and their families, local Jewish schools, camps, synagogues, and other Jewish community organizations. The Council also maintains and publishes the *North American Disability Resources Directory of Jewish Schools, Camps, Agencies, and Residential and Vocational Programs for the United States and Canada.* This directory can be obtained by going to their website, www.cjsn.org/Home.asp.

- Information about special needs camps, both Jewish and non-Jewish, can be obtained at the Developmental Disabilities page of the mysummercamps.com website. When you inquire about a specific camp, you may want to find out the approach to Judaism practiced at the camp, or you may want to assess your child's comfort level if the camp is not under Jewish auspices. Visit www.mysummercamps.com/camps/Special_Needs_Camps/Developmental_Disabilities/index.html.

Often overlooked is the side of the spectrum where gifted children can be found. Although gifted children can often function well in academic settings, they tend to be more isolated and socially less competent than their peers who fall within the "normal" range on the spectrum. Resources for families in this category include:

- The National Association for Gifted Children includes a parent section: www.nagc.com.
- Kidsource online: www.kidsource.com/kidsource/content/parents.gifted.html.
- Winner, Ellen. *Gifted Children: Myths and Realities.* New York: Basic Books, 1996.

Sexual Orientation

Even as our society moves toward a greater understanding and acceptance of homosexuality, major challenges still exist in a wide range of areas, both legal and social, for gay and lesbian adults today. For Jewish teens whose emerging sexuality may include homosexuality as a fact or as an inclination, the personal and emotional challenges can be even greater. The consequences of the struggle to identify and come to terms with a gay or lesbian sexual identity can be profound. According to the American Academy of Child and Adolescent Psychiatry, for example, recent studies indicate that "gay, lesbian and bisexual youth account for a significant number of deaths by suicide during adolescence."[1]

Feelings of attraction for persons of the same sex are not uncommon as sexual awareness emerges, experts say, and same-sex fantasies or experiences at this age do not conclusively demonstrate homosexuality, according to noted clinical psychologist and sex educator Dr. Sol Gordon, author of *When Living Hurts:* "All thoughts, dreams, and fantasies are normal—they come from the unconscious. If there is guilt about these fantasies, they will be repetitive; otherwise, they tend to pass." In our conversation, Dr. Gordon advised parents to let their adolescent children know that it is okay to have all kinds of sexual thoughts and feelings. He further suggests that parents encourage their adolescents to avoid making a final decision about homosexual orientation at this time in their lives, because experimentation does not equal sexual identity, which he believes is better determined in a person's early twenties. Dr. Gordon urges parents to always be open to conversation with their teens about any subject, especially one as important as sexual identity and orientation. "Be an 'askable' parent," he advises.

According to Dr. Daniel Chesir-Teran, assistant professor of family and children's studies at Montclair State University, since parents cannot predict the sexual orientation of their child at an early age, it is extremely important for all parents to be vigilant about the way they speak about subjects such as homosexuality. Children pick up on spoken words as well as unspoken attitudes very early on, and sending homophobic messages can result in emotional trauma for children who may later identify as gay or lesbian teenagers. "Parents must let their children know that their sexual orientation is okay, no matter what it is, and parents need to model decent, accepting behavior so that a gay or lesbian teen will not feel a fear of rejection in coming out to his or her own parents," he told me.

Dr. Chesir-Teran's own journey took him from the role of yeshiva boy in an Orthodox community to a gay male in a committed relationship with his partner, Ian. They are the parents of three adopted children. He believes that the fear of loss of family and loss of community that Jewish adolescents can experience at the thought of coming out contributes greatly to the anxiety and depression from which such young people can suffer. In addition, gay and lesbian adolescents often have very real fears about their physical safety. Parents should serve as advocates for their children and do everything in their power to let their teens know that love and support continue to be the defining terms of their relationship.

Negative attitudes in the Jewish community toward homosexuality stem from Leviticus 18:22 (the attitude toward lesbian relationships is markedly less severe). The Conservative Movement has been struggling with its stance on the issue of sexual orientation for some time, while both the Reform and the Reconstructionist Movements have embraced all Jews without regard to sexual orientation and have actively advocated for fair treatment and acceptance of gays, lesbians, and bisexual individuals. The major branches of

Judaism all agree on one point, however: every human being is created *b'tselem Elohim,* in God's image, regardless of sexual orientation.

From a Jewish parent's point of view, the road to acceptance of your child's gay or lesbian sexual orientation may be difficult. It may challenge your religious beliefs about the acceptability of homosexuality, and it may rattle you emotionally as you confront the multiple realities of having a gay or lesbian child. Seeking a support group or personal counseling may be helpful in navigating this transition. While you may want to encourage your teen to keep his or her mind open and not make any final decision about sexual orientation until after the teenage years, as Dr. Gordon suggests, mental health experts agree that it is unwise to try to force your child into a path of heterosexuality. Instead, focus on being open-minded, staying well informed, and being present in the deepest possible sense for your gay or lesbian teen, who needs all the love and the support that you can give.

Resources

- Balka, Christine, and Rose, Andy, eds. *Twice Blessed: On Being Lesbian, Gay, and Jewish.* Boston: Beacon Press, 1989.
- Downs, Alan. *The Velvet Rage: Overcoming the Pain of Growing Up Gay in a Straight Man's World.* Cambridge, MA: De Capo Press, 2005.
- www.keshetrabbis.org—This is a website for Conservative Movement rabbis who are supportive of gay and lesbian parents and families.
- www.outproud.org—The website of the National Coalition for Gay, Lesbian, Bisexual and Transgender Youth provides resources for youth and educators.
- www.pflag.org—PFLAG (Parents, Families, and Friends of Lesbians and Gays) supports gays and lesbians and their families through education and advocacy. Information about discussion and support groups can be accessed through their website.
- www.safeschoolscoalition.org/—This comprehensive website in support of gay, lesbian, bisexual, and transgender teens has many valuable links to helpful resources.

Adoption

In our tradition, being a parent is a supreme value. Our texts are crystal clear on this point. Procreation, rabbis tell us, is the very first mitzvah (commandment): "Be fruitful and multiply," God declares (Gen. 1:22). The Bible recounts numerous stories of women who either cannot bear children or who experience tremendous difficulty conceiving them, and in every case we feel the would-be mother's agony and desperation. On the first day of Rosh Hashanah, the haftarah selection (the reading from Prophets that follows the Torah reading) tells of the agony of a woman named Hannah, who cannot conceive and whose life seems meaningless to her without a child. Other biblical stories about women who have difficulty conceiving carry the same message, implicitly or explicitly: life is a misery if you cannot bear a child.

In modern times, the pain of childlessness is still acute for couples wishing to be parents. Judaism blesses the practice of adoption as a solution to this problem:

> Whoever brings up an orphan in his home is regarded, according to Scripture, as though the child had been born to him (BT, *Sanhedrin* 19b).

> He who brings up a child is to be called its father or mother, not the one who gave birth (Exodus *Rabbah,* ch. 46).

> If a person opens his door to another, that person is obligated to honor him more than his father and mother (Exodus *Rabbah,* ch. 4).

If you adopted a child who is now a Jewish teen, or about to become one, you have already traveled an emotional, legal, and psychological journey that others who haven't could not possibly understand. You may have made countless choices about how and whom to adopt, you may have engaged in great deliberation about when and what to tell your adopted child of his or her origins, or you may have decided to keep the adoption a secret. If you told your child about the adoption, you have probably had to deal with the ignorant and painful remarks of others that have hurt you and your child in ways not fully possible for others to understand ("So, do you know who your real mother is?").

If you chose to keep your child's origins a secret, then you may have lived with the fear of eventual discovery and the concern about how to address the situation, should that time ever come. I believe that secrecy, however well intended, is not the best course with children. Family secrets may be unspoken, but they often play out in unintended ways, so although we may think we are protecting our children from painful truths, we may actually be creating a situation in which open, honest dialogue is hampered on many levels. If your child is a teenager who does not know of his or her adoption, you may want to revisit this decision, but be sure to do so with the help of a mental health professional, because the teenage years are already a tumultuous time in terms of personal identity development.

If your child has been aware of his or her adoption all along, you may now find yourself at a time that you either dreaded or prepared for (or both): the interest in finding birth parents. Not every teen feels this need, but many do. This can feel quite threatening to adoptive parents, further complicating the already unsettling transition period the whole family is experiencing. Families who choose open adoptions can find, on the other hand, that rebellious teens may threaten to leave their adoptive parents so they can live with their birth parent(s).

The wisdom of adoptive parents who have weathered these storms is a striking model from which all parents can learn. Put your own fears and concerns aside, reach into your own soul to that place where the deepest love dwells, and focus on helping and supporting your child in every way you can. One parent of two adopted children shares this wisdom: "Encourage them to develop their identity, and don't inhibit them from finding out all the pieces of who they are. Communicate that they are free to be who they are, and love them regardless of what they choose." An adopted child who is now a rabbi puts it this way: "Give your children the freedom and the permission to do what they have to do, while maintaining the parental role. Deal with your own fear of losing your child, but don't put this on your child, because it's what often pushes children away. Have faith that the relationship you have had with your child will come back to you."

Resources

- Kapnek Rosenberg, Shelley. *Adoption and the Jewish Family.* Philadelphia: Jewish Publication Society, 1998.
- Kruger, Pamela, and Smolowe, Jill, eds. *A Love Like No Other: Stories from Adoptive Parents.* New York: Riverhead Books, 2005.
- www.starsofdavid.org/adoptee_resources.html—This is a comprehensive website that includes information and resources for adoptees by age group (school age, teens/young adults, and adults) as well as adoptive parents.

Divorce

Even the most well-crafted divorce agreements can't address the multitude of issues divorced parents face. As one dad explained, "Our divorce agreement was fifty-five pages long, and it still leaks like a sieve." Both the custodial and the noncustodial parent have special challenges they must address. In most cases, the custodial parent is the mother, who often finds herself in the demeaning position of having to secure financial support from an adversarial ex. The noncustodial parent, often the father, can feel shut out of the children's everyday life, causing many noncustodial parents to drift out of significant contact within three to four years of the divorce. Where joint custody is arranged, problems of being shuttled back and forth between two disrupted households can impact the children in unavoidable ways.

Divorced parents of Jewish teens face additional, painful challenges. The bar/bat mitzvah, otherwise a joyous celebration of achievement and coming of age, is often a nightmare for divorced families, with the emerging teenager in the middle. How is the aliyah (being called up to give the Torah blessing) of the parents to be handled? Who sits where? How are the other honors distributed? Who hosts the celebration, and are newer partners of either parent welcome? Trying to address these and myriad other important questions can, by all accounts, add more stress to an already stressful time.

According to the divorced parents with whom I have spoken, Jewish observance with teens becomes unusually difficult, if not impossible, after bar or bat mitzvah. "Jewish holidays and life-cycle events are horrible," shares one mom. "You lose things (Sabbath and holiday celebrations) because they are too hard to deal with," says another. A third mom reported that after her husband moved out, her three children refused to do the Friday-night Shabbat ritual they had always done as a family. "We can't do this without Dad," the children lamented. Although she initially forced the issue, she eventually gave up. A divorced father who is a rabbi recalled the difficulty of trying to balance his congregational responsibilities on Shabbat while at the same time trying to create a Sabbath home experience for his teen on the weekends she stayed with him.

For many families, differences in approaches to Jewish observance between the divorced parents are a cause of tension and stress for the children, who often find themselves caught in the middle of a battle for which they are not responsible. Sometimes the teen resorts to hurtful acting out ("You're not as Jewish as Dad: he keeps kosher and you don't"), and very often teens will take themselves out of the conflict entirely by dropping out of Jewish life in a way that can make parents, especially the custodial one, feel like a failure.

In general, the Jewish community has not done a good job of providing emotional support and assistance to divorced families. At the synagogue level, divorced parents of teens often complain of rabbis ill-equipped to counsel and support, an absence of helpful programming for them and their children, and an attitude that implicitly, if not explicitly, blames them for not being part of the "conventional" synagogue population, even though divorce is so common among our families today. Although federation-sponsored Jewish social service agencies may offer needed support groups, unfortunately these are often seen as "counseling," which, while important, does not address the normative social fabric of Jewish family life in the same way that synagogues and Jewish community centers might be able to do.

Given this landscape, what can divorced parents of Jewish teens do?

For the most part, you will have to take the initiative in reinventing your family's Jewish life in the best possible way. Here are some suggestions about how to accomplish this:

- Separate your anger at your ex, and the difficulties of your situation, from your behavior toward your teen. It is very important that you resist the natural temptation to react with anger to your teen, who is also reacting to the situation with anger. As best you can, try to see the world through your teen's eyes and try to help your child through the very bad moments in a way that doesn't pander by being overly permissive, but that reassures with a caring presence.

- Seize the opportunity to engage your soon-to-be-adult teen in frank and constructive discussions about what your new Jewish family life will be like. Conversations that demonstrate your respect for your teen under obviously challenging circumstances will provide a powerful model and will help reduce stress, while empowering your teen in a safe area of decision making.

- Transform old rituals into new, more doable ones. Some single-parent families create their own monthly Shabbat potluck dinners, though as we discussed earlier, it may be difficult to get your teen to join you. Console yourself with the fact that it is often just as difficult to keep teens engaged in home rituals in intact families. Since single parents who are involved in such groups report feelings of support and appreciation at continued Shabbat observance, this is definitely a course worth pursuing.

- "Acquire" a friend, the Talmud teaches us (*Pirkei Avot* 1:6). Now more than ever, you need a friend, or several, with whom to share your difficult moments as well as your triumphs. Use this as a starting point to begin your own support group, if need be. In this way, you'll be helping yourself as well as others. This is healing work.

- Advocate for programming in the synagogue and the JCC, and be prepared to take a leadership role. If you can identify the need for program support and can engage friends as volunteers in putting it together, you are likely to meet with better results. You have to be willing, though, to become involved and invest the effort to make it work.

In his powerfully insightful and healing book, *Divorce Is a Mitzvah: A Practical Guide to Finding Wholeness and Holiness When Your Marriage Dies* (Jewish Lights), Rabbi Perry Netter has this to share:

> When it feels as if you are surrounded by darkness and can't see your way clear, when it seems that your burdens are unbearable and you are about to collapse, know that this hardship is not forever. You will get through this, and life will again be full of joy. You will grow through this....
>
> Divorce is a mitzvah. Each step along the process introduces the opportunity to experience holiness. Each step includes the potential for bringing God's presence into the world. Embrace the sacred. For when you do, God will be with you. God will be with you through your darkest hour as your support, your companion, your guide. And God will be with you as you emerge into the light.[2]

Resources

- Netter, Perry. *Divorce Is a Mitzvah: A Practical Guide to Finding Wholeness and Holiness When Your Marriage Dies*. Woodstock, VT: Jewish Lights Publishing, 2002.

- "Dealing with Divorce," found at www.kidshealth.org/teen/ your_mind/Parents/divorce.html. An excellent article that explores the real world issues faced by teens whose parents are divorced or divorcing and offers constructive help.
- Long, Nicholas, and Forehand, Rex. *Making Divorce Easier on Your Child.* New York: McGraw-Hill Professional, 2002.

Interfaith Families

Below are resources that can be helpful in parenting Jewish children and teens in intermarried families or in families where the previously non-Jewish partner converted to Judaism.

- Keen, James. *Inside Intermarriage: A Christian Partner's Perspective on Raising a Jewish Family.* New York: URJ Press, 2006.
- Friedland, Ronnie, and Case, Edmund, eds. *The Guide to Jewish Interfaith Family Life: An InterfaithFamily.com Handbook.* Woodstock, VT: Jewish Lights Publishing, 2001.
- www.Interfaithfamily.com. A comprehensive website featuring articles on virtually every topic of interest to interfaith families.
- www.joi.org. The website of the Jewish Outreach Institute contains resources to help Jews and those married to Jews find a comfortable place within the Jewish community.
- urj.org/outreach. The website of the Union for Reform Judaism, Department of Outreach and Synagogue Community, offers a broad range of resources to those wishing to learn more about Judaism within the interfaith family setting.

Appendix B:
Situations That Require Intervention

This section contains suggestions that are general in nature. Parents whose teens exhibit involvement with risky or harmful behaviors and psychological disorders should consult appropriate medical or mental health experts in their community.

The teenage years are often a time when the struggle to assert independence and define individual identity results in behaviors that shock or alarm parents. Until fairly recently, we called these behaviors "teen rebellion," but today we are seeing something quite different—we are observing, or experiencing in our own families, adolescent behaviors that are truly dangerous. Although recent studies have shown that teens are "hardwired" to take risks, the number of teens who are engaging in dangerous and self-harming behaviors that require intervention is sharply rising.[1]

What are self-harmful behaviors, and how do we distinguish them from typical, innocent teen risk-taking? Is there a continuum, a point at which a certain behavior passes from normal teen experimentation to dangerous action? And as we are fighting our own internal parental emotional battle about letting go so we can let our child grow, how do we know when to keep silent and when to speak, when to overlook and when to intervene?

These are nuanced, complex questions. Before we try to develop answers, let's define a bit further what we are talking about when we speak of self-harming behaviors (some of which are symptoms of psychological illness). First, we can fairly easily say what such behaviors are *not:* they are not experimenting with alcohol, marijuana, or sexual activity in the later high school years. Although it is true that use of drugs and underage drinking are illegal and should never be encouraged or condoned by responsible parents, we do not classify limited, experimental use of alcohol or marijuana as self-harming behavior. These behaviors do, however, hold the potential to become self-harming, depending upon frequency and circumstances. For example, drinking or smoking marijuana often, alone, or both is risky, as is unprotected sex and sex outside of a committed, exclusive relationship. For our purposes, then, we will define risky and self-harming behaviors that require intervention as:

- Any involvement with cutting or other forms of self-mutilation
- Early involvement with alcohol; drugs, including marijuana; and sex
- Eating disorders
- Depression
- Suicidal tendencies

Teens engage in risky or self-harmful behaviors for a variety of reasons, though there do seem to be certain underlying causes. These are most often connected to low self-esteem and feelings of powerlessness, which can result from such earlier experiences as sexual abuse, unaddressed learning issues, and emotional or physical neglect. Harmful behaviors like cutting and eating disorders are symptoms of psychological illnesses, and, without help, a teen may not be able to control them. In general, teens who cut themselves do so because, after sealing themselves off emotionally to avoid painful feelings, they seek to experience *some* feeling—cutters often report that cutting makes them feel "alive" again. Early involvement with drugs, alcohol, and sex, on the other hand, can be ways of self-sedating or avoiding strong feelings of pain that may be experienced on an ongoing basis. Teens who engage in dysfunctional eating behaviors (anorexia and bulimia) do so for complicated and not fully understood reasons, though there seems to be some connection to feelings of worthlessness and powerlessness. Finally, depression and suicidal tendencies both reflect feelings of hopelessness and futility.

What should parents of Jewish teens do to prevent dangerous, self-harmful behaviors in their children, or to address such problems if they already exist? If you are already in a crisis situation, that is to say, if your child is already engaging in behaviors that put him or her at serious risk, *it is imperative that you get immediate professional help to ensure your child's physical safety.* This point cannot be emphasized strongly enough—do not worry about annoying, alienating, or embarrassing your child at this moment. I can assure you, I have done all of that, as my children will grumpily tell you, when I had reason to think that their health or safety was at risk. Keeping your kid safe is a parent's most fundamental job, and you are bound to make some mistakes in judgment along the way. Err on the side of safety, because the alternative is too horrible to contemplate. Involve doctors, mental health professionals, guidance counselors, rabbis, youth group advisors, or anyone close at hand who can help you take immediate measures, and do not hesitate to go to any lengths necessary to save your child. When the crisis moment passes, continue to involve the professionals mentioned here and consult the end of this Appendix for additional resources for your family, because the road to recovery from risky or self-harming behaviors and psychological disorders is often a long and difficult one.

Lately, we have been seeing in the Jewish community an increasing number of adolescents engaging in risky and self-harming behaviors that are not necessarily connected to early trauma or obvious neglect. Instead, these young people are feeling overwhelmed by the stresses and pressures of their daily lives. Experts who work with Jewish teens and their families report that the academic expectations parents place on their children from an early age, coupled with implicit or explicit messages about how successful the teens must be, regardless of the capabilities of the individual children, are creating an emotional environment where feelings of failure, rather than self-worth, are increasingly the teen's reality. According to Rabbi Edythe

Mencher of the Union for Reform Judaism's Department of Jewish Family Concerns, "There is a stress for perfection that makes kids feel they are not special. The message we often send is: 'Be better, be better, what you're doing is not enough.' The need to achieve is at an extraordinary level." Parents, she points out, are themselves under similar pressure to achieve, and how they respond teaches their children how to handle such stress. Eating, drinking, and avoidance-of-intimacy issues in parents create negative models for teens, who may learn to turn to risky or harmful behaviors as a way of self-soothing. "These may provide temporary relief in the short term," Rabbi Mencher says, "but these measures never solve the real problems, and they end up creating additional ones." Psychologist and educator Dr. Sol Gordon puts it this way: "Sometimes parents forget that adolescents need models more than they need critics."[2]

How can we help our teenagers recover from crisis, or avoid it altogether, so they can function productively in their world? Our odds for this outcome, and for a healthier future beyond the teenage years, are enormously increased if we can provide them with these essential assets:

- Love and acceptance. There are times when it feels incredibly difficult to demonstrate love and acceptance of your teen, especially when the child is engaging in behavior that you frankly find repugnant. Much of the time, though, we reject our teens emotionally or judge them too harshly for far less serious reasons, such as poor grades, failure to excel at sports, choices in dress, and so on. Either way, it's incumbent upon us to work at changing our own behavior so we can help our children grow. People are quick to recommend therapy for teens, and I don't disagree, but I'm quicker to recommend therapy for parents, or family therapy. Sometimes, there is no good alternative to doing that work on ourselves if we truly want to give our children what they deserve from us, and from life.

- Feelings of being valued. It takes time to make a relationship work. Even when teens seem to push us away, they really want our presence and caring, in the many ways we demonstrate these things. There's no getting around the fact that this requires time and attention on our part. Material gifts and the benefits of affluence do not ultimately make people feel valued; only our positive, constructive presence can engender that feeling in our teenagers.

- Involvement with positive risk-taking behaviors. Teens are risk-taking creatures, but not all risks are negative ones, as Stephen G. Wallace, the chairman and chief executive officer of SADD (Students Against Destructive Decisions) points out: "Teens in particular are likely to take risks in order to assert their individuality and independence. Significantly, creating meaningful opportunities for positive risk-taking can not only decrease the likelihood of negative risk-taking but can also satisfy a developmentally driven appetite to try new things and to make new discoveries about themselves and the world around them."[3] Examples of positive risk-taking behavior include volunteering to teach younger children, becoming involved in community-service projects, speaking out against bullying behavior and encouraging others to do the same, engaging in a new activity, or learning a new skill.

- A caring, meaningful community. We live in a world that can often seem fragmented and threatening, and feelings of loneliness and vulnerability are experienced by teens, parents, and young children alike. In 2003, the findings were published from a study conducted by the YMCA, Dartmouth Medical School, and the Institute for American Values about at-risk children and teens. The report, as previously mentioned, is called *Hardwired to Connect: The New Scientific Case for Authoritative Communities.* It outlined the need for the creation of authoritative communities to nurture and support children, teens, and families to counteract the deteriorating mental and behavioral health of children in our country today. The report lists ten main characteristics of such communities, including "is warm and nurturing, establishes clear limits and expectations, is multigenerational, reflects and transmits a shared understanding of what it means to be a good person, encourages spiritual and religious development, is philosophically oriented to the equal dignity of all persons and to the principle of love of neighbor."[4] Sounds a lot like what our synagogues could be.

In the final analysis, we as parents must find the way to give our teens the tools they need to be successful. Risky and self-harming behaviors are not ends in themselves; they are the reflection of problems and/or illnesses that lie beneath the surface, and they are problems we cannot afford to ignore. Judaism teaches us that we are created *b'tzelem Elohim,* in God's image, and our job is to reflect this vision in our parenting to help our teens move toward that vision themselves. Rabbi Richard Address, who has spearheaded the Reform Movement's groundbreaking *Kedushat HaGuf* (the sanctity of the body) initiative to raise consciousness and find solutions to teen self-harming behaviors, puts it quite directly: "What people crave most in relationships is love, intimacy, connection. What we need to communicate to our teens is, 'We love you, God loves you, you are safe and respected and valued here.'" Based on all the work he has done in this area, what does he think is the bottom line? His answer applies to every parent of a Jewish teen: "Love your kid, all the rest is commentary."

Resources

- www.coolnurse.com/self-injury.htm—This very helpful site, with information that explains the phenomenon of self-harming behaviors, provides resources as well as personal stories from those who have engaged in these behaviors.
- www.sadd.org—The website of Students Against Destructive Decisions (originally Students Against Drunk Driving) provides a wide range of information and resources for students, parents, and professionals.
- www.urj.org/jfc—The website of the Department of Jewish Family Concerns of the Union for Reform Judaism contains helpful information about a range of risky and self-destructive behaviors.

Appendix C:
Parenting Jewish Teens Program

Introduction

The Parenting Jewish Teens program was designed to be offered in a synagogue or Jewish community center setting, and it can easily be adapted to other group settings as well. Because the program can operate on so many levels, expertise on the part of the program leader is desirable in a number of disciplines, including education, family dynamics, group processes, and Jewish literacy. Given the broad range of skills required to most successfully lead the program, two facilitators may be better than one in some cases.

The purpose of the Parenting Jewish Teens program is to help parents explore challenging issues and offer support and guidance within the Jewish community. Ideally, an ongoing group might be created to help parents through the difficult transition from children as children to children as young adults. The session that follows is an example of what could be used as a onetime program or as a kickoff for a longer-term series. In the latter case, participants might be invited to set the agenda, or organizers can utilize a predetermined topical outline using the chapters in this book as a guide.

A Parenting Jewish Teens program has the potential to:

- Keep parents connected to the synagogue after the bar/bat mitzvah of their children
- Provide a supportive environment—a sanctuary—for families during one of life's most challenging transitions
- Send the message to parents that today's synagogues and Jewish community centers are places of meaning and relevance for them at every stage of their lives

It is important to acknowledge that the full range of teen behaviors includes some that are potentially very serious, such as drug and alcohol use/abuse, early sex, unsafe sex, eating disorders, and self-mutilation. Although this parent education session is not designed to address these issues in a substantive way, it is important that the facilitator be aware of the resources available in the community to help families facing these kinds of situations, and be able to offer referrals, where appropriate.

Session Overview

Introductions (5–10 minutes)

Identifying Difficult Issues (10 minutes)

Messages from Biblical Models (10 minutes)

Jewish Parenting Continuum—What Can Parents Do? (10 minutes)

Addressing Difficult Issues (15–20 minutes)

Conclusion (5–10 minutes)

Materials/Resources Needed

- A comfortable room for adults with seats that can be rearranged
- A blackboard and chalk or flip chart, markers, and tape
- Copies of the Text Study and Background for Texts sheets (see pages 136–138)
- A timely bibliography and relevant magazine or newspaper articles for sharing with the group
- Refreshments for participants

Session Plan

Introductions (5–10 minutes)

Some introductory remarks should precede the personal introductions. It is often useful to put the program in context; for example, explain why a session like this is being offered at this time, what the expressed or perceived need for it has been, etc. A relaxed, nonthreatening environment should be established at this point, and participants should be notified that confidentiality is crucial to protect everyone's privacy: what is said in the group should stay in the group.

Identifying Difficult Issues (10 minutes)

Ask parents to express their frustrations, fears, and concerns regarding their teenagers. Listen carefully as parents speak, and note their issues on the flip chart or blackboard. Typical entries might include: messy room; fresh talk; insufficient attention to schoolwork; laziness; opposition to Jewish observance, especially synagogue attendance; irresponsibility about spending money; and the like. If parents do not include an issue that you believe may really be one, such as sex, drugs, and alcohol, suggest it and see what the reaction is.

Do not try to address the issues now—this is an issues identification exercise. Instead, you can reflect on the list that has been created by saying something like: "We've gotten a lot of issues on the table, and I sense there were moments of great recognition and consensus among many parents present. Let's move on, keeping these issues in mind. We will return to them later in the session."

Messages from Biblical Models (10 minutes)

In this activity, parents have an opportunity to look at three biblical texts that each describe leaving home in a different way. If you believe that your group is likely to be somewhat familiar with these texts, you can just proceed in accordance with the directions below. If not, explain that they will be looking at three texts from the

Torah, the first five books of the Hebrew Bible. You may also want to distribute copies of the Background for Texts sheet, which follows the Text Study sheet (see page 137).

1. Distribute the Text Study sheet and ask participants to review the texts in groups of two or three to try to discern a common theme. After they have read and discussed the texts, ask the groups to write a title for them as if they were three one-act plays. Reconvene the whole group and invite participants to share their thoughts about what the common theme might be and their titles for three one-act plays.

2. Point out or confirm that each of the biblical stories presents a separation issue. Although some separations are painful and destructive, what was the ultimate outcome of the separation stories depicted in the texts? (Each of these biblical figures underwent a positive transformation after he left home.)

3. Explain that, as the texts suggest, separation is important for the child, but how does it feel for parents, at least today? Ask the participants to share their answers and write key words on the blackboard or flip chart.

4. Mention that, in our society, the period of adolescence is so extended that the separation process takes place, at least in part, while teenagers are still living with us. How we handle it can have a direct effect on feelings and relationships for years to come. Share with the group that the feelings of loss and sadness many parents experience as their children move toward independence are often unconscious and are sometimes expressed in "parental acting out." An important goal is to acknowledge and deal with these feelings and work toward constructive behaviors.

Jewish Parenting Continuum—What Can Parents Do? *(10 minutes)*

In this learning activity, parents identify key elements of their relationship with their children when the children were young and are then asked to share a vision of how they would ideally like to describe the relationship with their children when the children become adults. Finally, they consider the "middle," the teenage years, and reflect upon how they, the parents, must change to enable their children to grow.

1. Copy and distribute the following three texts and ask volunteers to read them one at a time, followed by reactions and discussion. The group might be asked to address the question: What are the implications of this text for our parenting?

I.

All husbands and wives borrow their children. Our children are not our own; our children belong to God.... They are not ours to keep, but to rear. They are not given to us to mold into our image. They are not given to us so that we can force them to fulfill our lives and thus, in some way, cancel our failures. They are not tools to be used, but souls to be loved. [Thomas C. Short, quoted in Chaim Stern, ed. *Day to Day: Reflections on the Themes in the Torah from Literature, Philosophy, and Religious Thought* (New York: CCAR Press, 1998), p. 281.]

II.

Alas for the children who are exiled from their parents' table. Alas for the parents who have exiled their children. [Adapted from Babylonian Talmud, *Berachot* 3a.]

III.

A man once complained to the Ba'al Shem Tov, the founder of Chasidism, about his son. The youth had turned away from religion. "What shall I do, Rebbe?" asked the distraught man. "Do you love your son?" "Of course I do." "Then love him even more." [Tale about Rabbi Israel ben Eliezer, c. 1700, in Francine Klagsbrun, *Voices of Wisdom: Jewish Ideals and Ethics for Everyday Living* (Middle Village, NY: Jonathan David Publishers, 1980), p. 186.]

2. Ask the group: How would we characterize the relationship we had with our children when they were little? The responses can be written on one side of the blackboard/flip chart. Typical answers include: "Dependency; thinking I was perfect, invincible; having control over my child's behavior."

3. Next, ask the group: How do we envision the relationship with our children when they become adults? Responses should be written on the other side of the blackboard/flip chart, leaving space in between. Typical "visions" include: "Independence; accepting me for who I really am; hoping for a good relationship as adults together; able to lead a happy life and still be close with our family; affiliated with Jewish life."

4. Pose the question: How do we get from here to there? Since the teenage years are a transition period, how does parental behavior have to change to help teenagers grow into the adults we have described above? The empty space in the middle of the blackboard/flip chart represents this transition. You may want to use the "Jewish Parenting Continuum" diagram in Chapter 7 to help you with this. Ask participants to write at least one behavior of theirs that they might change to help their teen move more peacefully into Jewish adulthood. Reflective answers to this question might include: "I have to listen more carefully to what he is saying," "I have to gradually give her more control over her life," "I have to involve him more in the decision making about family issues that affect him."

Addressing Difficult Issues (15–20 minutes)

Parents are asked to work in groups to develop strategies for addressing the issues that were articulated at the beginning of the session. A goal of this activity is to demonstrate, through experiential processing, that parents are able to find their own answers, especially when working within a supportive, caring community, such as the one this group represents.

1. Ask parents to refer back to the list of difficult issues the group compiled earlier in the session. Ask them to vote for the *two* issues that they believe to be of most pressing concern for them. Record the number of votes for each issue. Determine which three issues receive the greatest number of votes. Divide the participants into three groups, and assign each group one of the three issues. If the number of participants is small, it may be more comfortable to do this activity as a whole group.

2. Ask each group to discuss the issue it has been assigned and to take approximately ten minutes to develop several constructive strategies for addressing it.

3. Bring the groups back together and ask them to report on the constructive strategies they developed. Record these on the flip chart or board, or ask a volunteer to do so. You may want to share the following general strategies that some parents of teens find helpful:

   • Learn from people who have been there: groups like these, people with slightly older children, books, and other resources.
   • Celebrate your successes. Find reasons to have fun.
   • Be there for your child and just listen.
   • Remember the time-out system and use it—for yourself! Sometimes parents need a time-out; don't be afraid to take it.

4. Ask parents to reflect on the process of working with one another to develop strategies for addressing their issues—how did it feel?

5. Congratulate them for their good work!

Conclusion (5–10 minutes)

If this session is the beginning of a series, ask participants to brainstorm the topics they would like to address in the remaining sessions. In any case, point out to them the great value of working together and supporting one another during the sometimes turbulent years of parenting Jewish teens.

Conclude the program by asking the participants to answer the following questions:

- What did you find most helpful or interesting about today's program?
- If you could change one thing about the program, what would it be?

Distribute any handouts that you have and thank the participants for coming.

Text Study

Text #1

The Lord said to Abram [later renamed Abraham], "Go forth from your native land and from your father's house to the land that I will show you. I will make of you a great nation, and I will bless you. I will make your name great, and you shall be a blessing...." Abram went forth as the Lord had commanded him (Gen. 12:1–4).

Text #2

Now Esau harbored a grudge against Jacob because of the blessing which his father [Isaac] had given him, and Esau said to himself, "Let but the mourning period of my father come, and I will kill my brother Jacob." When the words of her older son Esau were reported to Rebekah, she sent for her younger son Jacob and said to him, "Your brother Esau is consoling himself by planning to kill you. Now, my son, listen to me. Flee at once to Haran, to my brother Laban. Stay with him a while, until your brother's fury subsides and he forgets what you have done to him" (Gen. 27:41–45).

Text #3

They [Joseph's brothers] saw him from afar, and before he came close to them they conspired to kill him. They said to one another,

"Here comes that dreamer! Come now, let us kill him and throw him into one of the pits; and we can say, 'A savage beast devoured him.'" ... Then Judah said to his brothers, "What do we gain by killing our brother and covering up his blood? Come, let us sell him to the Ishmaelites...." His brothers agreed. When Midianite traders passed by, they pulled Joseph up out of the pit. They sold Joseph for twenty pieces of silver to the Ishmaelites, who brought Joseph to Egypt (Gen. 18:20, 26–28).

Text translations are taken from *Etz Hayim Torah and Commentary,* edited by David L. Lieber (Philadelphia: Jewish Publication Society, 2001).

Background for Texts

Text #1

Abram, later renamed Abraham, was the son of Terah, and he was married to Sarai, who was later renamed Sarah. Abram-Abraham was to become the first Jew and the first monotheist (believer in one God). Abraham and Sarah would become the first patriarch and matriarch of the Jewish people. Their physical journey is thus often seen as a spiritual one as well. Abraham is remembered for his absolute faith in God, as demonstrated on at least two occasions: first, when he unquestioningly follows God's command to uproot his family and to travel to an unidentified destination, and second, when he prepares to offer his beloved son, Isaac, as a sacrifice in response to God's instruction.

Text #2

Jacob and Esau were twins, born to Isaac and Rebekah. Isaac favored Esau, the firstborn, who was a hunter and a woodsman. Rebekah favored Jacob. During her pregnancy, God had told her that each son would lead a nation and that "one people shall be mightier than the other, and the older shall serve the younger" (Gen. 25:23).

As Isaac lay ailing and almost blind, Rebekah convinced Jacob to disguise himself and pretend to be his older brother, Esau, so that Isaac would be tricked into giving Jacob the birthright (i.e., the inheritance).

Text #3

Jacob had two wives and female servants with whom he fathered children. His second wife, Rachel, was his real love. After many barren years, she finally gave birth to a son, Joseph. Rachel died while giving birth to a second son, Benjamin. Jacob's unabashed favoritism of Joseph over his eleven brothers is popularly known through the story of the beautiful multicolored coat that Jacob gave to Joseph. That, together with Joseph's tendency to flaunt his special status, inspired intense sibling hatred toward him among his brothers.

Notes

Preface

1. The word *Torah* means "teaching," and refers in its narrowest sense to the first five books of the Hebrew Bible, which contain accounts of the beginning of the world and the early stories of the Israelites, as well as the 613 commandments that provide the basis for the later development of Jewish law (Halacha). In its larger sense, the term refers to the entirety of Jewish religious and legal thought and practice.

2. The Talmud is a legal code based on the teachings of the Bible. The Talmud was developed over the course of approximately six hundred years and is comprised of two main divisions: the Mishnah, which represents the teachings, commentaries, and interpretations that were transmitted orally until about 200 CE, and the Gemarah, which contains additional teachings, commentaries, and interpretations on the Mishnah by later scholars. Two Talmuds developed—the Palestinian Talmud and the Babylonian Talmud; the latter is more widely cited.

Chapter I

1. The professional literature in the field of family dynamics contains references to the "dip" in marital happiness during the middle years, when children living in the home are teenagers. See, for example, Laurence Steinberg and Susan B. Silverberg, "Influences on Marital Satisfaction during the Middle Stages of the Family Life Cycle," in *Journal of Marriage and the Family,* November, 1987, 49 (4): pp. 751–760.

2. Anthony E. Wolf, *Get Out of My Life, but first could you drive me and Cheryl to the mall?* rev. ed. (New York: Farrar, Straus and Giroux, 2002), p. 4.

3. Arthur Green, *These Are the Words: A Vocabulary of Jewish Spiritual Life* (Woodstock, VT: Jewish Lights Publishing, 1999), p. 142.

4. *The Simpsons,* www.thesimpsons.com/characters (accessed on November 6, 2005).

5. Robert D. Putnam, *Bowling Alone: The Collapse and Revival of American Community* (New York: Simon & Schuster, 2000), p. 287.

6. Steven M. Cohen and Arnold M. Eisen, *The Jew Within: Self, Family, and Community in America* (Bloomington, IN: Indiana University Press, 2000), p. 7.

7. Commission on Children at Risk, *Hardwired to Connect: The New Scientific Case for Authoritative Communities* (New York: Institute for American Values, 2003), p. 5.

8. Norman J. Cohen, *Hineini in Our Lives: Learning How to Respond to Others through 14 Biblical Texts and Personal Stories* (Woodstock, VT: Jewish Lights Publishing, 2003), p. xi.

Chapter 2

1. The word *hasid* comes from the term *hesed,* which refers to an unbounded love and generosity of spirit. The Hasidic movement as we know it today originated in Eastern Europe in the mid-eighteenth century and centered around the teachings of a charismatic, mystical rabbi, Israel ben Eliezer, known as the Ba'al Shem Tov ("Master of the Good Name"). Hasidism began as an emotional, spiritual response to a Judaism that had become intensely focused on scholarship and thereby out of reach for the everyday Jew. The Ba'al Shem Tov and his followers believed that connection with God was possible as a joyous, soulful experience that transcended text-based learning. Initially anti-establishment, Hasidism in our time fits within the fold of ultra-Orthodoxy and has incorporated disciplined study as a value alongside religious ecstasy.

Chapter 3

1. Jonathan D. Sarna, *American Judaism: A History* (New Haven: Yale University Press, 2004), p. 371.

2. See www.pbs.org/wgbh/pages/frontline/shows/teenbrain/.

3. Linda Sonna, *The Everything Parenting a Teenager Book: A Survival Guide for Parents!* (Avon, MA: Adams Media, 2004), p. 7.

4. Carla K. Johnson, "Young teens view oral sex as less risky than intercourse, study finds," in *Associated Press,* April 3, 2005, www.ap.org/ (accessed April 4, 2005).

5. Ron Taffel, *The Second Family: How Adolescent Power Is Challenging the American Family* (New York: St. Martin's Press, 2001), p. 17.

6. The RAND Corporation, "Does Watching Sex on Television Influence Teens' Sexual Activity?" www.rand.org/pubs/research_briefs/RB9068/index1.html

(accessed April 6, 2005). According to its website, the RAND Corporation is the original nonprofit think tank helping to improve policy and decision making through objective research and analysis.

7. The RAND Corporation, "Teenage Alcohol Misuse: A Big Problem and a Different Solution," www.rand.org/pubs/research_briefs/RB6004-1/index1. html (accessed April 6, 2005).

8. "Underage Drinkers Starting at Earlier Age," CNN.com, February 27, 2002, http://archives.cnn.com/2002/HEALTH/parenting/02/26/teen.drinking/index.html (accessed April 6, 2005).

9. "Parents Attitudes Toward Drinking Influence Children's Behavior," Jewish Community Federation of Louisville, www.jewishlouisville.org (accessed April 6, 2005).

10. Grace Palladino, "The Concept of Teenagers Created a Marketing Niche," in *The American Teenager: Examining Pop Culture,* ed. Kate Burns (Farmington Hills, MI: Greenhaven, 2003), p. 33.

11. Barrie Gunter, "Does Media Sex Influence Young People?" in *The American Teenager: Examining Pop Culture,* ed. Kate Burns (Farmington Hills, MI: Greenhaven, 2003), p. 123.

12. Sharon Begley, "A World of Their Own," *Newsweek,* May 8, 2000, p. 54.

13. Taffel, *The Second Family,* p. 17.

14. Howard Good, "Wilderness Road: Schooling with Too Few Counselors, Too Little 'Friendly Interest,'" in *Education Week,* August 11, 2004, p. 56.

15. Charles Kadushin et al., "Being a Jewish Teenager in America: Trying to Make It" (Waltham, MA: The Cohen Center for Modern Jewish Studies, Brandeis University, 2000), p. vii.

16. Some efforts are now being made within the synagogue communities to address teen sexual behavior issues. These include the Union for Reform Judaism's Sacred Choices curriculum (www.urj.org/sacredchoices) and a curriculum focusing on sexuality, abusive relationships, and teen violence that is being developed by the Jewish Theological Seminary.

17. Johanna Ginsberg, "In School and On Line, Yeshiva Students, Educators Address the Reality of Substance Abuse," in *New Jersey Jewish News,* December 9, 2004.

18. Ibid., "Area High Schools Respond to Arrest of Teens at Livingston Party," in *New Jersey Jewish News,* November 25, 2004, www.njjewishnews.com/njjn.com/112504/mwarrest.html (accessed on April 6, 2005).

19. Ibid.

20. Ilana Kramer, "Teen Sex That's 'No Big Deal,'" in *Lilith,* Winter, 2003, pp. 16–18.

Chapter 4

1. The *Amidah* ("standing") is the central prayer recited in a Jewish worship service, either public or private. It contains three sections: Blessings of Praise, Blessings of Petition, and Blessings of Thanksgiving. Variations to this structure and to the blessings that are said occur on the Shabbat and on holidays. This prayer is also referred to as the *Shemoneh Esreh* (Eighteen) because of the eighteen benedictions it originally contained.

2. Elaine Kahn, "Conservative Movement Issuing New Texts to Answer New Needs," in *New Jersey Jewish News,* December 17, 1998.

3. *The Random House Dictionary of the English Language: The Unabridged Edition* (New York: Random House, 1967), p. 308.

4. Mel Levine, *Ready or Not, Here Life Comes* (New York: Simon and Schuster, 2005), p. 45.

5. Gary J. Niels, "Forum: Corporate cheating: lessons from the classroom," Post-gazette.com, August 4, 2002, www.postgazette.com/forum/comm/20020804edniels0804p1.asp (accessed September 9, 2004).

6. Moses Maimonides, *Misheh Torah, Hilchot De'ot* 2:3.

7. Aharon Yaakov Greenberg, ed., *Torah Gems,* vol. 2, trans. Shmuel Himelstein (Tel Aviv, Israel: Yavneh Publishing House, 1998), p. 316.

8. Rick Warren, *The Purpose-Driven Life: What on Earth Am I Here For?* (Grand Rapids, MI: Zondervan, 2002), p. 147.

Chapter 5

1. The Kaddish prayer appears in several versions in the synagogue service. *Kaddish Yatom* has come to be known as a memorial prayer for the dead, though it is really a statement of praise for God, and death is never mentioned.

2. Unpublished translation of original Hebrew found in Aharon Yaakov Greenberg, ed., *Torah Gems,* vol. 3 (Tel Aviv, Israel: Yavneh Publishing House, 1995), p. 210.

3. Wendy Mogel, "The Present Parent," in *Reform Judaism,* Summer 2004, vol. 32 (4): p. 49.

4. Covenant here refers to the contractual agreement between the Jewish people and God. Although the Bible suggests several covenantal moments between individuals (e.g., Abraham) and God, the concept of covenant also applies to the entire Jewish people throughout history as a consequence of the acceptance of Torah at Mount Sinai.

5. A ceremony called *pidyon haben* (redemption of the son) in which Jewish parents "buy back" their firstborn son, who was traditionally dedicated to the service of the Temple.

6. The trained Jew (often a rabbi or cantor) who performs the ritual act of circumcision on a Jewish baby boy on his eighth day of life.

7. Although Jewish baby girls entered the community in a more private way by simply being given a Hebrew name, an increasing number of communities these days are encouraging parents to hold a public baby-naming ceremony and celebration for girls, usually in the synagogue.

8. Shlomo Riskin, *The Passover Haggadah with a Traditional and Contemporary Commentary by Shlomo Riskin* (New York: KTAV, 1983), p. 9.

9. Author's translation of Solomon Ganzfried, *Code of Jewish Law: A Compilation of Jewish Laws and Customs,* annotated rev. ed., vol. 4 (New York: Hebrew Publishing Co., 1963), p. 1.

10. Robert Kegan, *In Over Our Heads: The Mental Demands of Modern Life* (Cambridge, MA: Harvard University Press, 1995), p. 81.

11. Nanci Hellmich, "Parents Want to Be Teens' Pals," in *USA Today,* October 12, 2004.

12. Francine Klagsburn, *Voices of Wisdom: Jewish Ideals and Ethics for Everyday Living* (Middle Village, NY: Jonathan David Publishers, 1980), p. 179.

13. Chaim Stern, ed., *Gates of Repentance: The New Union Prayerbook for the Days of Awe,* rev. ed. (New York: CCAR Press, 1996), p. 328.

14. Harvey J. Fields, *A Torah Commentary for Our Times,* vol. 1 (New York: UAHC Press, 1990), p. 67.

15. Ibid.

16. Ibid.

17. Abraham J. Twerski, *I Didn't Ask to Be in This Family: Sibling Relationships and How They Shape Adult Behavior and Dependencies* (New York: Topper Books, 1992), p. 21.

18. Zelig Pliskin, *Guard Your Tongue: A Practical Guide to the Laws of Loshon Hora* (Union City, NJ: Gross Bros. Printing, 1975).

19. Even in the stories of reconciliation between Esau and Jacob, and later, Joseph and his brothers, a certain amount of tension seems to linger in the text.

20. Riskin, *The Passover Haggadah,* p. 53.

21. Translations from ibid., pp. 55–60.

22. Menahem Hakohen and Hayim Ron, eds., *The Passover Seder: Legends and Customs* (New York: Adama Books, 1987), p. 10.

Chapter 6

1. W. Gunther Plaut and David E. S. Stein, eds., *The Torah: A Modern Commentary,* rev. ed. (New York: URJ Press, 2005), p. 1239–40.

2. Tale about Rabbi Israel ben Eliezer in Francine Klagsbrun, *Voices of Wisdom,* p. 186.

3. Hilary Stout, "Family Dinners Improve Kids' Health, Grades; How Not to Dread Them," in *Wall St. Journal,* November 11, 2004.

4. See Charles Kadushin et al., "Being a Jewish Teenager in America," pp. 57–66.

Chapter 7

1. Linda Sonna, *The Everything Parenting a Teenager Book,* p. 39.

2. Robert Brooks, "'Is It Ever Too Late?'—Nurturing Positive Mindsets Throughout Our Lives," Resilience, Self-Esteem, Motivation, and Family Relationships, http://drrobertbrooks.com/writings/articles/0501.html (accessed April 30, 2006).

3. Thomas C. Short, quoted in *Day to Day: Reflections on the Themes in the Torah from Literature, Philosophy, and Religious Thought,* Chaim Stern, ed. (New York: CCAR Press, 1998), p. 281. Reprinted with permission of the CCAR Press.

4. Bradley Shavit Artson, "Released from Responsibility," in *Today's Torah,* electronic newsletter from the Ziegler Rabbinic School, University of Judaism (Ziegler School-*Parashat Toldot* 5765, November 13, 2004).

Chapter 8

1. Selected study findings can be found at www.ujc.org/content_display. html?ArticleID=83911.

2. Sylvia Barack Fishman, *Double or Nothing? Jewish Families and Mixed Marriage* (Lebanon, NH: Brandeis University Press, 2004), p. 59.

Chapter 9

1. Quoted in Lawrence Kushner, *God was in this Place and I, i did not know: Finding Self, Spirituality, and Ultimate Meaning* (Woodstock, VT: Jewish Lights Publishing, 1991), p. 165.

2. Green, *These Are the Words,* p. 137.

3. The term actually used is *al chet,* which is often conveniently translated as "sin" but means something far different, though not so easily translated. *Al chet* means to miss the mark, as in a target that has not been achieved. In terms of our behavior, we can think of the things we strive for, the ways in which we want to be better parents, spouses, partners, children, friends, citizens, and members of our community, and we acknowledge our "misses," our failures to act in accordance with our ideals. This doesn't mean we are evil or bad, only that we have to try harder in the year to come.

4. Michael Walzer, *Exodus and Revolution* (Cambridge, MA: Basic Books, 1985), p. 149. Reprinted with permission of Basic Books, a member of Perseus Books, L.C., Cambridge, MA.

5. The idea of a relationship between parenting and *tikkun olam* was inspired by the title of a parent education lesson ("Parenting Is *Tikkun Olam*") in the Reform Movement's *CHAI: Learning for Jewish Life* curriculum. The lesson was written by Barbara Binder Kadden.

6. Martin Buber, *The Later Masters*, quoted in Ellen Frankel, *The Classic Tales: 4,000 Years of Jewish Lore* (Northvale NJ: Jason Aronson Inc., 1989).

7. *Hardwired to Connect*, p. 5.

8. Thomas Friedman, *The World Is Flat: A Brief History of the Twenty-first Century* (New York: Farrar, Straus and Giroux, 2005), pp. 303, 305.

9. Levine, *Ready or Not,* p. 46.

10. *Hardwired to Connect,* p. 15.

Appendix A

1. "Gay, Lesbian and Bisexual Adolescents," No. 63 (revised November 2005), American Academy of Child and Adolescent Psychology, www.aacap.org/publications/factsfam/63.htm (accessed April 30, 2006).

2. Perry Netter, *Divorce Is a Mitzvah: A Practical Guide to Finding Wholeness and Holiness When Your Marriage Dies* (Woodstock, VT: Jewish Lights Publishing, 2002), p. 187.

Appendix B

1. Stephen G. Wallace, "The Myth of Risk: Promoting Healthy Behavior by Challenging Teens," Students Against Destructive Decisions, www.sadd.org/pdf/Myth_of_Risk_Camping.pdf (accessed April 30, 2006).

2. Sol Gordon, *When Living Hurts,* rev. ed. (New York: URJ Press, 2004), p. 116.

3. Stephen G. Wallace, "The Myth of Risk."

4. *Hardwired to Connect,* p. 34.

Selected Bibliography

This bibliography contains books and articles that were of particular significance in the preparation of this book and others that are likely to be of further interest to the reader.

Amsel, Nachum. *The Jewish Encyclopedia of Moral and Ethical Issues.* Northvale, NJ: Jason Aronson, Inc., 1996.

Beaudoin, Tom. *Virtual Faith: The Irreverent Spiritual Quest of Generation X.* San Francisco: Jossey Bass, 1998.

Begley, Sharon. "A World of Their Own," *Newsweek,* May 8, 2000.

Bradley, Michael. *Yes, Your Teen Is Crazy: Loving Your Kid without Losing Your Mind.* Gig Harbor, WA: Harbor Press, 2003.

Brooks, Robert. "'Is It Ever Too Late?'—Nurturing Positive Mindsets Throughout Our Lives," http://drrobertbrooks.com/writings/articles/0501.html.

Brooks, Robert, and Sam Goldstein. *Raising Resilient Children.* New York: Contemporary Books, 2001.

Brownlee, Shannon. "Inside the Teen Brain," *U.S. News & World Report,* August 9, 1999, pp. 45–54.

Burns, Kate, ed. *The American Teenager: Examining Pop Culture.* Farmington Hills, MI: Greenhaven, 2003.

Cohen, Norman J. *Hineini in Our Lives: Learning How to Respond to Others through 14 Biblical Texts and Personal Stories.* Woodstock, VT: Jewish Lights Publishing, 2003.

Cohen, Steven M., and Arnold M. Eisen. *The Jew Within: Self, Family, and Community in America.* Bloomington, IN: Indiana University Press, 2000.

Commission on Children at Risk. *Hardwired to Connect: The New Scientific Case for Authoritative Communities.* Institute for American Values, New York, 2003.

Craig, Judi. *You're Grounded Till You're Thirty!* New York: Hearst Books, 1996.

Elias, Maurice J., et al. *Raising Emotionally Intelligent Teenagers.* New York: Harmony Books, 2000.

Evans, Robert. *Family Matters: How Schools Can Cope with the Crisis in Childrearing.* San Francisco: Jossey-Bass, 2004.

Fields, Harvey J. *A Torah Commentary for Our Times.* New York: UAHC Press, 1991.

Friedman, Thomas. *The World Is Flat: A Brief History of the Twenty-first Century.* New York: Farrar, Straus, & Giroux, 2005.

Ganzfried, Solomon. *Code of Jewish Law: A Compilation of Jewish Laws and Customs,* annotated rev. ed. New York: Hebrew Publishing Company, 1963.

Gates of Repentance: The New Union Prayerbook for the Days of Awe (New York: CCAR Press, 1978, rev. 1996).

"Gay and Lesbian Adolescents," No. 63, revised November 2005, American Academy of Child and Adolescent Psychology, www.aacap.org/publications/factsfam/63.htm.

Ginsberg, Johanna. "In School and On Line, Yeshiva Students, Educators Address the Reality of Substance Abuse," *New Jersey Jewish News,* www.njjewishnews.com/njjn.com/120904/njinschool.html, accessed April 6, 2005.

Gordon, Sol, and Judith Gordon. *When Living Hurts,* rev. ed. New York: URJ Press, 2004.

———. *Raising a Child Responsibly in a Sexually Permissive World,* 2nd. ed. Avon, MA: Adams Media Corporation, 2000.

Green, Arthur. *These Are the Words: A Vocabulary of Jewish Spiritual Life.* Woodstock, VT: Jewish Lights Publishing, 1999.

HaKohen, Menachem, and Ron, Hayim, eds. *The Passover Seder: Legends and Customs.* New York: Adama Books, 1987.

Kegan, Robert. *In Over Our Heads: The Mental Demands of Modern Life.* Cambridge, MA: Harvard University Press, 1995.

Kindlon, Dan. *Raising Cain: Protecting the Emotional Life of Boys.* New York: Ballantine Books, 1999.

Klagsburn, Francine. *Voices of Wisdom: Jewish Ideals and Ethics for Everyday Living.* Middle Village, NY: Jonathan David Publishers, 1980.

Kushner, Lawrence. *God was in this Place and I, i did not know: Finding Self, Spirituality and Ultimate Meaning.* Woodstock, VT: Jewish Lights Publishing, 1991.

Levine, Mel. *Ready or Not, Here Life Comes.* New York: Simon and Schuster, 2005.

Mogel, Wendy. "The Present Parent," in *Reform Judaism,* Summer 2004.

———. *Blessings of a Skinned Knee.* New York: Penguin Compass, 2001.

Netter, Perry. *Divorce Is a Mitzvah: A Practical Guide to Finding Wholeness and Holiness When Your Marriage Dies.* Woodstock, VT: Jewish Lights Publishing, 2002.

Plaut, W. Gunther, and Stein, David E. S., eds. *The Torah: A Modern Commentary,* rev. ed. New York: URJ Press, 2005.

Pliskin, Zelig. *Guard Your Tongue: A Practical Guide to the Laws of Loshon Hora.* Union City, NJ: Gross Bros. Printing Co. Inc., 1975.

Putnam, Robert D. *Bowling Alone: The Collapse and Revival of American Community.* New York: Simon & Schuster, 2000.

Riskin, Shlomo. *The Passover Haggadah with a Traditional and Contemporary Commentary.* New York: KTAV Publishing, 1983.

Sachs, Brad E. *The Good Enough Teen.* New York: HarperCollins, 2005.

Sarna, Jonathan D. *American Judaism: A History.* New Haven: Yale University Press, 2004.

Search Institute. "Parenting at the Speed of Teens: Positive Tips on Everyday Issues." Minneapolis, MN: Search Institute, 2004.

Sonna, Linda. *The Everything Parenting a Teenager Book: A Survival Guide for Parents!* Avon, MA: Adams Media, 2004.

Stern, Chaim, ed. *Day to Day: Reflections on the Themes in the Torah.* New York: CCAR Press, 1998.

Stout Hilary. "Family Dinners Improve Kids' Health, Grades; How Not to Dread Them." *Wall Street Journal,* November 11, 2004.

Taffel, Ron. *The Second Family: How Adolescent Power Is Challenging the American Family.* New York: St. Martin's Press, 2001.

Telushkin, Joseph. *Jewish Wisdom: Ethical, Spiritual, and Historical Lessons from the Great Works and Thinkers.* New York: William Morrow and Company, 1994.

Twerski, Abraham J. *I Didn't Ask to Be in This Family: Sibling Relationships and How They Shape Adult Behavior and Dependencies.* New York: Topper Books, 1992.

Warren, Rick. *The Purpose-Driven Life: What on Earth Am I Here For?* Grand Rapids, MI: Zondervan, 2002.

Wolf, Anthony E. *Get Out of My Life, but first could you drive me and Cheryl to the mall?* rev. ed. New York: Farrar, Straus, and Giroux, 2002.

———. *The Secret of Parenting: How to Be in Charge of Today's Kids—from Toddlers to Preteens—without Threats or Punishment.* New York: Farrar, Straus, and Giroux, 2000.

AVAILABLE FROM BETTER BOOKSTORES.
TRY YOUR BOOKSTORE FIRST.

Current Events/History

The Story of the Jews: A 4,000-Year Adventure—A Graphic History Book
Written & illustrated by Stan Mack
Witty, illustrated narrative of all the major happenings from biblical times to the twenty-first century. 6 x 9, 288 pp, illus., Quality PB, 978-1-58023-155-8 **$16.95**

Hannah Senesh: Her Life and Diary, the First Complete Edition
By Hannah Senesh; Foreword by Marge Piercy; Preface by Eitan Senesh
6 x 9, 352 pp, HC, 978-1-58023-212-8 **$24.99**

The Jewish Prophet: Visionary Words from Moses and Miriam to Henrietta Szold and A. J. Heschel *By Rabbi Dr. Michael J. Shire*
6½ x 8½, 128 pp, 123 full-color illus., HC, 978-1-58023-168-8
Special gift price $14.95

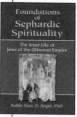

Foundations of Sephardic Spirituality: The Inner Life of Jews of the Ottoman Empire
By Rabbi Marc D. Angel, PhD 6 x 9, 224 pp, HC, 978-1-58023-243-2 **$24.99**

Judaism and Justice: The Jewish Passion to Repair the World
By Rabbi Sidney Schwarz
6 x 9, 352 pp, HC, 978-1-58023-312-5 **$24.99**

Grief/Healing

Against the Dying of the Light: A Parent's Story of Love, Loss and Hope
By Leonard Fein
5½ x 8½, 176 pp, Quality PB, 978-1-58023-197-8 **$15.99**

Grief in Our Seasons: A Mourner's Kaddish Companion *By Rabbi Kerry M. Olitzky*
4½ x 6½, 448 pp, Quality PB, 978-1-879045-55-2 **$15.95**

Healing of Soul, Healing of Body: Spiritual Leaders Unfold the Strength & Solace in Psalms *Edited by Rabbi Simkha Y. Weintraub, CSW*
6 x 9, 128 pp, 2-color illus. text, Quality PB, 978-1-879045-31-6 **$14.99**

Jewish Paths toward Healing and Wholeness: A Personal Guide to Dealing with Suffering *By Rabbi Kerry M. Olitzky; Foreword by Debbie Friedman.*
6 x 9, 192 pp, Quality PB, 978-1-58023-068-1 **$15.95**

Mourning & Mitzvah, 2nd Edition: A Guided Journal for Walking the Mourner's Path through Grief to Healing *By Anne Brener, LCSW*
7½ x 9, 304 pp, Quality PB, 978-1-58023-113-8 **$19.99**

The Perfect Stranger's Guide to Funerals and Grieving Practices
A Guide to Etiquette in Other People's Religious Ceremonies *Edited by Stuart M. Matlins*
6 x 9, 240 pp, Quality PB, 978-1-893361-20-1 **$16.95** *(A SkyLight Paths book)*

Tears of Sorrow, Seeds of Hope: A Jewish Spiritual Companion for Infertility and Pregnancy Loss *By Rabbi Nina Beth Cardin*
6 x 9, 192 pp, HC, 978-1-58023-017-9 **$19.95**

A Time to Mourn, A Time to Comfort, 2nd Edition: A Guide to Jewish Bereavement *By Dr. Ron Wolfson*
7 x 9, 384 pp, Quality PB, 978-1-58023-253-1 **$19.99**

When a Grandparent Dies: A Kid's Own Remembering Workbook for Dealing with Shiva and the Year Beyond *By Nechama Liss-Levinson, PhD*
8 x 10, 48 pp, 2-color text, HC, 978-1-879045-44-6 **$15.95** *For ages 7–13*

Or phone, fax, mail or e-mail to: **JEWISH LIGHTS** Publishing
Sunset Farm Offices, Route 4 • P.O. Box 237 • Woodstock, Vermont 05091
Tel: (802) 457-4000 • Fax: (802) 457-4004 • www.jewishlights.com
Credit card orders: **(800) 962-4544** (8:30AM–5:30PM ET Monday–Friday)
Generous discounts on quantity orders. SATISFACTION GUARANTEED. Prices subject to change.

Theology/Philosophy/The Way Into... Series

The Way Into... series offers an accessible and highly usable "guided tour" of the Jewish faith, people, history and beliefs—in total, an introduction to Judaism that will enable you to understand and interact with the sacred texts of the Jewish tradition. Each volume is written by a leading contemporary scholar and teacher, and explores one key aspect of Judaism. *The Way Into...* series enables all readers to achieve a real sense of Jewish cultural literacy through guided study.

The Way Into Encountering God in Judaism

By Neil Gillman
For everyone who wants to understand how Jews have encountered God throughout history and today.
6 x 9, 240 pp, Quality PB, 978-1-58023-199-2 **$18.99**; HC, 978-1-58023-025-4 **$21.95**
Also Available: **The Jewish Approach to God:** A Brief Introduction for Christians
By Neil Gillman
5½ x 8½, 192 pp, Quality PB, 978-1-58023-190-9 **$16.95**

The Way Into Jewish Mystical Tradition

By Lawrence Kushner
Allows readers to interact directly with the sacred mystical text of the Jewish tradition. An accessible introduction to the concepts of Jewish mysticism, their religious and spiritual significance and how they relate to life today.
6 x 9, 224 pp, Quality PB, 978-1-58023-200-5 **$18.99**; HC, 978-1-58023-029-2 **$21.95**

The Way Into Jewish Prayer

By Lawrence A. Hoffman
Opens the door to 3,000 years of Jewish prayer, making available all anyone needs to feel at home in the Jewish way of communicating with God.
6 x 9, 224 pp, Quality PB, 978-1-58023-201-2 **$18.99**

The Way Into Judaism and the Environment

By Jeremy Benstein
Explores the ways in which Judaism contributes to contemporary social-environmental issues, the extent to which Judaism is part of the problem and how it can be part of the solution.
6 x 9, 288 pp, HC, 978-1-58023-268-5 **$24.99**

The Way Into *Tikkun Olam* (Repairing the World)

By Elliot N. Dorff
An accessible introduction to the Jewish concept of the individual's responsibility to care for others and repair the world.
6 x 9, 320 pp, HC, 978-1-58023-269-2 **$24.99**

The Way Into Torah

By Norman J. Cohen
Helps guide in the exploration of the origins and development of Torah, explains why it should be studied and how to do it.
6 x 9, 176 pp, Quality PB, 978-1-58023-198-5 **$16.99**; HC, 978-1-58023-028-5 **$21.95**

The Way Into the Varieties of Jewishness

By Sylvia Barack Fishman, PhD
Explores the religious and historical understanding of what it has meant to be Jewish from ancient times to the present controversy over "Who is a Jew?"
6 x 9, 288 pp, HC, 978-1-58023-030-8 **$24.99**

Inspiration

God's To-Do List: 103 Ways to Be an Angel and Do God's Work on Earth
By Dr. Ron Wolfson 6 x 9, 144 pp, Quality PB, 978-1-58023-301-9 **$15.99**

God in All Moments: Mystical & Practical Spiritual Wisdom from Hasidic Masters
Edited and translated by Or N. Rose with Ebn D. Leader
5½ x 8½, 192 pp, Quality PB, 978-1-58023-186-2 **$16.95**

Our Dance with God: Finding Prayer, Perspective and Meaning in the Stories of Our
Lives *By Karyn D. Kedar* 6 x 9, 176 pp, Quality PB, 978-1-58023-202-9 **$16.99**
Also Available: **The Dance of the Dolphin** (HC edition of *Our Dance with God*)
6 x 9, 176 pp, HC, 978-1-58023-154-1 **$19.95**

The Empty Chair: Finding Hope and Joy—Timeless Wisdom from a Hasidic Master,
Rebbe Nachman of Breslov *Adapted by Moshe Mykoff and the Breslov Research Institute*
4 x 6, 128 pp, 2-color text, Deluxe PB w/flaps, 978-1-879045-67-5 **$9.95**

The Gentle Weapon: Prayers for Everyday and Not-So-Everyday Moments—
Timeless Wisdom from the Teachings of the Hasidic Master, Rebbe Nachman of Breslov
Adapted by Moshe Mykoff and S. C. Mizrahi, together with the Breslov Research Institute
4 x 6, 144 pp, 2-color text, Deluxe PB w/flaps, 978-1-58023-022-3 **$9.99**

God Whispers: Stories of the Soul, Lessons of the Heart *By Karyn D. Kedar*
6 x 9, 176 pp, Quality PB, 978-1-58023-088-9 **$15.95**

An Orphan in History: One Man's Triumphant Search for His Jewish Roots
By Paul Cowan; Afterword by Rachel Cowan. 6 x 9, 288 pp, Quality PB, 978-1-58023-135-0 **$16.95**

Restful Reflections: Nighttime Inspiration to Calm the Soul, Based on Jewish Wisdom
By Rabbi Kerry M. Olitzky & Rabbi Lori Forman 4½ x 6½, 448 pp, Quality PB, 978-1-58023-091-9 **$15.95**

Sacred Intentions: Daily Inspiration to Strengthen the Spirit, Based on Jewish Wisdom
By Rabbi Kerry M. Olitzky and Rabbi Lori Forman 4½ x 6½, 448 pp, Quality PB, 978-1-58023-061-2 **$15.95**

Kabbalah/Mysticism/Enneagram

Awakening to Kabbalah: The Guiding Light of Spiritual Fulfillment
By Rav Michael Laitman, PhD 6 x 9, 192 pp, HC, 978-1-58023-264-7 **$21.99**

Seek My Face: A Jewish Mystical Theology *By Arthur Green*
6 x 9, 304 pp, Quality PB, 978-1-58023-130-5 **$19.95**

Zohar: Annotated & Explained
Translation and annotation by Daniel C. Matt; Foreword by Andrew Harvey
5½ x 8½, 176 pp, Quality PB, 978-1-893361-51-5 **$15.99** *(A SkyLight Paths book)*

Cast in God's Image: Discover Your Personality Type Using the Enneagram and Kabbalah
By Rabbi Howard A. Addison
7 x 9, 176 pp, Quality PB, Layflat binding, 20+ journaling exercises, 978-1-58023-124-4 **$16.95**

Ehyeh: A Kabbalah for Tomorrow
By Arthur Green 6 x 9, 224 pp, Quality PB, 978-1-58023-213-5 **$16.99**

The Enneagram and Kabbalah, 2nd Edition: Reading Your Soul
By Rabbi Howard A. Addison 6 x 9, 192 pp, Quality PB, 978-1-58023-229-6 **$16.99**

Finding Joy: A Practical Spiritual Guide to Happiness *By Dannel I. Schwartz with Mark Hass*
6 x 9, 192 pp, Quality PB, 978-1-58023-009-4 **$14.95**

The Flame of the Heart: Prayers of a Chasidic Mystic *By Reb Noson of Breslov. Translated by*
David Sears with the Breslov Research Institute 5 x 7¼, 160 pp, Quality PB, 978-1-58023-246-3 **$15.99**

The Gift of Kabbalah: Discovering the Secrets of Heaven, Renewing Your Life on Earth
By Tamar Frankiel, PhD 6 x 9, 256 pp, Quality PB, 978-1-58023-141-1 **$16.95;**
HC, 978-1-58023-108-4 **$21.95**

Kabbalah: A Brief Introduction for Christians
By Tamar Frankiel, PhD 5½ x 8½, 208 pp, Quality PB, 978-1-58023-303-3 **$16.99**

The Lost Princess and Other Kabbalistic Tales of Rebbe Nachman of Breslov
The Seven Beggars and Other Kabbalistic Tales of Rebbe Nachman of Breslov
Translated by Rabbi Aryeh Kaplan; Preface by Rabbi Chaim Kramer
Lost Princess: 6 x 9, 400 pp, Quality PB, 978-1-58023-217-3 **$18.99**
Seven Beggars: 6 x 9, 192 pp, Quality PB, 978-1-58023-250-0 **$16.99**

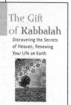

See also *The Way Into Jewish Mystical Tradition* in Spirituality / The Way Into... Series

Meditation

The Handbook of Jewish Meditation Practices
A Guide for Enriching the Sabbath and Other Days of Your Life
By Rabbi David A. Cooper Easy-to-learn meditation techniques.
6 x 9, 208 pp, Quality PB, 978-1-58023-102-2 **$16.95**

Discovering Jewish Meditation: Instruction & Guidance for Learning an Ancient
Spiritual Practice *By Nan Fink Gefen*
6 x 9, 208 pp, Quality PB, 978-1-58023-067-4 **$16.95**

A Heart of Stillness: A Complete Guide to Learning the Art of Meditation
By David A. Cooper 5½ x 8½, 272 pp, Quality PB, 978-1-893361-03-4 **$16.95** *(A SkyLight Paths book)*

Meditation from the Heart of Judaism: Today's Teachers Share Their
Practices, Techniques, and Faith *Edited by Avram Davis*
6 x 9, 256 pp, Quality PB, 978-1-58023-049-0 **$16.95**

Silence, Simplicity & Solitude: A Complete Guide to Spiritual Retreat at Home
By David A. Cooper 5½ x 8½, 336 pp, Quality PB, 978-1-893361-04-1 **$16.95**
(A SkyLight Paths book)

The Way of Flame: A Guide to the Forgotten Mystical Tradition of Jewish
Meditation *By Avram Davis* 4½ x 8, 176 pp, Quality PB, 978-1-58023-060-5 **$15.95**

Ritual/Sacred Practice/Journaling

The Jewish Dream Book: The Key to Opening the Inner Meaning of
Your Dreams *By Vanessa L. Ochs with Elizabeth Ochs; Full-color illus. by Kristina Swarner*
Instructions for how modern people can perform ancient Jewish dream practices
and dream interpretations drawn from the Jewish wisdom tradition.
8 x 8, 128 pp, Full-color illus., Deluxe PB w/flaps, 978-1-58023-132-9 **$16.95**

The Jewish Journaling Book: How to Use Jewish Tradition to Write
Your Life & Explore Your Soul *By Janet Ruth Falon*
Details the history of Jewish journaling throughout biblical and modern times, and
teaches specific journaling techniques to help you create and maintain a vital journal,
from a Jewish perspective. 8 x 8, 304 pp, Deluxe PB w/flaps, 978-1-58023-203-6 **$18.99**

The Book of Jewish Sacred Practices: CLAL's Guide to Everyday & Holiday
Rituals & Blessings *Edited by Rabbi Irwin Kula and Vanessa L. Ochs, PhD*
6 x 9, 368 pp, Quality PB, 978-1-58023-152-7 **$18.95**

Jewish Ritual: A Brief Introduction for Christians
By Rabbi Kerry M. Olitzky and Rabbi Daniel Judson
5½ x 8½, 144 pp, Quality PB, 978-1-58023-210-4 **$14.99**

The Rituals & Practices of a Jewish Life: A Handbook for Personal Spiritual
Renewal *Edited by Rabbi Kerry M. Olitzky and Rabbi Daniel Judson*
6 x 9, 272 pp, illus., Quality PB, 978-1-58023-169-5 **$18.95**

The Sacred Art of Lovingkindness: Preparing to Practice
By Rabbi Rami Shapiro 5½ x 8½, 176 pp, Quality PB, 978-1-59473-151-8 **$16.99**
(A SkyLight Paths book)

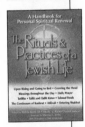

Science Fiction/Mystery & Detective Fiction

Mystery Midrash: An Anthology of Jewish Mystery & Detective Fiction
Edited by Lawrence W. Raphael; Preface by Joel Siegel
6 x 9, 304 pp, Quality PB, 978-1-58023-055-1 **$16.95**

Criminal Kabbalah: An Intriguing Anthology of Jewish Mystery & Detective Fiction
Edited by Lawrence W. Raphael; Foreword by Laurie R. King
6 x 9, 256 pp, Quality PB, 978-1-58023-109-1 **$16.95**

Wandering Stars: An Anthology of Jewish Fantasy & Science Fiction
Edited by Jack Dann; Introduction by Isaac Asimov
6 x 9, 272 pp, Quality PB, 978-1-58023-005-6 **$16.95**

More Wandering Stars: An Anthology of Outstanding Stories of Jewish Fantasy and
Science Fiction *Edited by Jack Dann; Introduction by Isaac Asimov*
6 x 9, 192 pp, Quality PB, 978-1-58023-063-6 **$16.95**

Spirituality

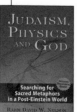

The Adventures of Rabbi Harvey: A Graphic Novel of Jewish Wisdom and Wit in the Wild West *By Steve Sheinkin*
Jewish and American folktales combine in this witty and original graphic novel collection. Creatively retold and set on the western frontier of the 1870s.
6 x 9, 144 pp, Full-color illus., Quality PB, 978-1-58023-310-1 **$16.99**
Also Available: **The Adventures of Rabbi Harvey Teacher's Guide**
8½ x 11, 32 pp, PB, 978-1-58023-326-2 **$8.99**

Ethics of the Sages: Pirke Avot—Annotated & Explained
Translation and Annotation by Rabbi Rami Shapiro
5½ x 8½, 192 pp, Quality PB, 978-1-59473-207-2 **$16.99** *(A SkyLight Paths book)*

A Book of Life: Embracing Judaism as a Spiritual Practice
By Michael Strassfeld 6 x 9, 528 pp, Quality PB, 978-1-58023-247-0 **$19.99**

Meaning and Mitzvah: Daily Practices for Reclaiming Judaism through Prayer, God, Torah, Hebrew, Mitzvot and Peoplehood *By Rabbi Goldie Milgram*
7 x 9, 336 pp, Quality PB, 978-1-58023-256-2 **$19.99**

The Soul of the Story: Meetings with Remarkable People
By Rabbi David Zeller 6 x 9, 288 pp, HC, 978-1-58023-272-2 **$21.99**

Aleph-Bet Yoga: Embodying the Hebrew Letters for Physical and Spiritual Well-Being
By Steven A. Rapp. Foreword by Tamar Frankiel, PhD and Judy Greenfeld. Preface by Hart Lazer.
7 x 10, 128 pp, b/w photos, Quality PB, Layflat binding, 978-1-58023-162-6 **$16.95**

Entering the Temple of Dreams: Jewish Prayers, Movements, and Meditations for the End of the Day *By Tamar Frankiel, PhD, and Judy Greenfeld*
7 x 10, 192 pp, illus., Quality PB, 978-1-58023-079-7 **$16.95**

Does the Soul Survive? A Jewish Journey to Belief in Afterlife, Past Lives & Living with Purpose *By Rabbi Elie Kaplan Spitz; Foreword by Brian L. Weiss, MD*
6 x 9, 288 pp, Quality PB, 978-1-58023-165-7 **$16.99**

First Steps to a New Jewish Spirit: Reb Zalman's Guide to Recapturing the Intimacy & Ecstasy in Your Relationship with God *By Rabbi Zalman M. Schachter-Shalomi with Donald Gropman* 6 x 9, 144 pp, Quality PB, 978-1-58023-182-4 **$16.95**

God in Our Relationships: Spirituality between People from the Teachings of Martin Buber *By Rabbi Dennis S. Ross* 5½ x 8½, 160 pp, Quality PB, 978-1-58023-147-3 **$16.95**

Judaism, Physics and God: Searching for Sacred Metaphors in a Post-Einstein World
By Rabbi David W. Nelson 6 x 9, 368 pp, Quality PB, inc. reader's discussion guide, 978-1-58023-306-4 **$18.99**;
HC, 352 pp, 978-1-58023-252-4 **$24.99**

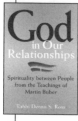

The Jewish Lights Spirituality Handbook: A Guide to Understanding, Exploring & Living a Spiritual Life *Edited by Stuart M. Matlins*
What exactly is "Jewish" about spirituality? How do I make it a part of my life? Fifty of today's foremost spiritual leaders share their ideas and experience with us.
6 x 9, 456 pp, Quality PB, 978-1-58023-093-3 **$19.99**

Bringing the Psalms to Life: How to Understand and Use the Book of Psalms
By Daniel F. Polish 6 x 9, 208 pp, Quality PB, 978-1-58023-157-2 **$16.95**;
HC, 978-1-58023-077-3 **$21.95**

God & the Big Bang: Discovering Harmony between Science & Spirituality
By Daniel C. Matt 6 x 9, 216 pp, Quality PB, 978-1-879045-89-7 **$16.99**

Minding the Temple of the Soul: Balancing Body, Mind, and Spirit through Traditional Jewish Prayer, Movement, and Meditation *By Tamar Frankiel, PhD, and Judy Greenfeld*
7 x 10, 184 pp, illus., Quality PB, 978-1-879045-64-4 **$16.95**
Audiotape of the Blessings and Meditations: 60 min. **$9.95**
Videotape of the Movements and Meditations: 46 min. **$20.00**

One God Clapping: The Spiritual Path of a Zen Rabbi *By Alan Lew with Sherril Jaffe*
5½ x 8½, 336 pp, Quality PB, 978-1-58023-115-2 **$16.95**

There Is No Messiah ... and You're It: The Stunning Transformation of Judaism's Most Provocative Idea *By Rabbi Robert N. Levine, DD*
6 x 9, 192 pp, Quality PB, 978-1-58023-255-5 **$16.99**

These Are the Words: A Vocabulary of Jewish Spiritual Life
By Arthur Green 6 x 9, 304 pp, Quality PB, 978-1-58023-107-7 **$18.95**

Spirituality/Lawrence Kushner

Filling Words with Light: Hasidic and Mystical Reflections on Jewish Prayer
By Lawrence Kushner and Nehemia Polen
5½ x 8½, 176 pp, HC, 978-1-58023-216-6 **$21.99**

The Book of Letters: A Mystical Hebrew Alphabet
Popular HC Edition, 6 x 9, 80 pp, 2-color text, 978-1-879045-00-2 **$24.95**
Collector's Limited Edition, 9 x 12, 80 pp, gold foil embossed pages, w/limited edition silkscreened print, 978-1-879045-04-0 **$349.00**

The Book of Miracles: A Young Person's Guide to Jewish Spiritual Awareness
6 x 9, 96 pp, 2-color illus., HC, 978-1-879045-78-1 **$16.95** *For ages 9 and up*

The Book of Words: Talking Spiritual Life, Living Spiritual Talk
6 x 9, 160 pp, Quality PB, 978-1-58023-020-9 **$16.95**

Eyes Remade for Wonder: A Lawrence Kushner Reader   *Introduction by Thomas Moore*
6 x 9, 240 pp, Quality PB, 978-1-58023-042-1 **$18.95**

God Was in This Place & I, i Did Not Know: Finding Self, Spirituality and Ultimate Meaning   6 x 9, 192 pp, Quality PB, 978-1-879045-33-0 **$16.95**

Honey from the Rock: An Introduction to Jewish Mysticism
6 x 9, 176 pp, Quality PB, 978-1-58023-073-5 **$16.95**

Invisible Lines of Connection: Sacred Stories of the Ordinary
5½ x 8½, 160 pp, Quality PB, 978-1-879045-98-9 **$15.95**

Jewish Spirituality—A Brief Introduction for Christians
5½ x 8½, 112 pp, Quality PB, 978-1-58023-150-3 **$12.95**

The River of Light: Jewish Mystical Awareness
6 x 9, 192 pp, Quality PB, 978-1-58023-096-4 **$16.95**

The Way Into Jewish Mystical Tradition
6 x 9, 224 pp, Quality PB, 978-1-58023-200-5 **$18.99**; HC, 978-1-58023-029-2 **$21.95**

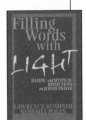

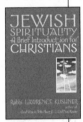

Spirituality/Prayer

Pray Tell: A Hadassah Guide to Jewish Prayer
By Rabbi Jules Harlow, with contributions from many others
8½ x 11, 400 pp, Quality PB, 978-1-58023-163-3 **$29.95**

Witnesses to the One: The Spiritual History of the *Sh'ma* By Rabbi Joseph B. Meszler;
Foreword by Rabbi Elyse Goldstein 6 x 9, 176 pp, HC, 978-1-58023-309-5 **$19.99**

My People's Prayer Book Series
Traditional Prayers, Modern Commentaries   *Edited by Rabbi Lawrence A. Hoffman*
Provides diverse and exciting commentary to the traditional liturgy, helping modern men and women find new wisdom in Jewish prayer, and bring liturgy into their lives. Each book includes Hebrew text, modern translation, and commentaries from all perspectives of the Jewish world.

Vol. 1—The *Sh'ma* and Its Blessings
7 x 10, 168 pp, HC, 978-1-879045-79-8 **$24.99**

Vol. 2—The *Amidah*
7 x 10, 240 pp, HC, 978-1-879045-80-4 **$24.95**

Vol. 3—*P'sukei D'zimrah* (Morning Psalms)
7 x 10, 240 pp, HC, 978-1-879045-81-1 **$24.95**

Vol. 4—*Seder K'riat Hatorah* (The Torah Service)
7 x 10, 264 pp, HC, 978-1-879045-82-8 **$23.95**

Vol. 5—*Birkhot Hashachar* (Morning Blessings)
7 x 10, 240 pp, HC, 978-1-879045-83-5 **$24.95**

Vol. 6—*Tachanun* and Concluding Prayers
7 x 10, 240 pp, HC, 978-1-879045-84-2 **$24.95**

Vol. 7—Shabbat at Home
7 x 10, 240 pp, HC, 978-1-879045-85-9 **$24.95**

Vol. 8—*Kabbalat Shabbat* (Welcoming Shabbat in the Synagogue)
7 x 10, 240 pp, HC, 978-1-58023-121-3 **$24.99**

Vol. 9—Welcoming the Night: *Minchah* and *Ma'ariv* (Afternoon and Evening Prayer) 7 x 10, 272 pp, HC, 978-1-58023-262-3 **$24.99**

Vol. 10—Shabbat Morning: *Shacharit* and *Musaf* (Morning and Additional Services) 7 x 10, 240 pp, HC, 978-1-58023-240-1 **$24.99**

Spirituality/Women's Interest

The Quotable Jewish Woman: Wisdom, Inspiration & Humor from the Mind & Heart
Edited and compiled by Elaine Bernstein Partnow
6 x 9, 496 pp, HC, 978-1-58023-193-0 **$29.99**

The Knitting Way: A Guide to Spiritual Self-Discovery *By Linda Skolnick and Janice MacDaniels* 7 x 9, 240 pp, Quality PB, 978-1-59473-079-5 **$16.99** *(A SkyLight Paths book)*

The Quilting Path: A Guide to Spiritual Self-Discovery through Fabric, Thread and Kabbalah
By Louise Silk 7 x 9, 192 pp, Quality PB, 978-1-59473-206-5 **$16.99** *(A SkyLight Paths book)*

The Divine Feminine in Biblical Wisdom Literature: Selections Annotated & Explained *Translated and Annotated by Rabbi Rami Shapiro*
5½ x 8½, 240 pp, Quality PB, 978-1-59473-109-9 **$16.99** *(A SkyLight Paths book)*

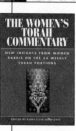

Lifecycles, Vol. 1: Jewish Women on Life Passages & Personal Milestones
Edited and with Introductions by Rabbi Debra Orenstein
6 x 9, 480 pp, Quality PB, 978-1-58023-018-6 **$19.95**

Lifecycles, Vol. 2: Jewish Women on Biblical Themes in Contemporary Life
Edited and with Introductions by Rabbi Debra Orenstein and Rabbi Jane Rachel Litman
6 x 9, 464 pp, Quality PB, 978-1-58023-019-3 **$19.95**

Moonbeams: A Hadassah Rosh Hodesh Guide *Edited by Carol Diament, PhD*
8½ x 11, 240 pp, Quality PB, 978-1-58023-099-5 **$20.00**

ReVisions: Seeing Torah through a Feminist Lens *By Rabbi Elyse Goldstein*
5½ x 8½, 224 pp, Quality PB, 978-1-58023-117-6 **$16.95**

The Women's Haftarah Commentary: New Insights from Women Rabbis on the 54 Weekly Haftarah Portions, the 5 Megillot & Special Shabbatot
Edited by Rabbi Elyse Goldstein 6 x 9, 560 pp, HC, 978-1-58023-133-6 **$39.99**

The Women's Torah Commentary: New Insights from Women Rabbis on the 54 Weekly Torah Portions *Edited by Rabbi Elyse Goldstein*
6 x 9, 496 pp, HC, 978-1-58023-076-6 **$34.95**

The Year Mom Got Religion: One Woman's Midlife Journey into Judaism
By Lee Meyerhoff Hendler 6 x 9, 208 pp, Quality PB, 978-1-58023-070-4 **$15.95**

See Holidays for *The Women's Passover Companion: Women's Reflections on the Festival of Freedom* and *The Women's Seder Sourcebook: Rituals & Readings for Use at the Passover Seder*. Also see Bar/Bat Mitzvah for *The JGirl's Guide: The Young Jewish Woman's Handbook for Coming of Age*.

Travel

Israel—A Spiritual Travel Guide, 2nd Edition
A Companion for the Modern Jewish Pilgrim
By Rabbi Lawrence A. Hoffman 4¾ x 10, 256 pp, Quality PB, illus., 978-1-58023-261-6 **$18.99**

Also Available: **The Israel Mission Leader's Guide** 978-1-58023-085-8 **$4.95**

12-Step

100 Blessings Every Day: Daily Twelve Step Recovery Affirmations, Exercises for Personal Growth & Renewal Reflecting Seasons of the Jewish Year
By Rabbi Kerry M. Olitzky; Foreword by Rabbi Neil Gillman
4¼ x 6¼, 432 pp, Quality PB, 978-1-879045-30-9 **$15.99**

Recovery from Codependence: A Jewish Twelve Steps Guide to Healing Your Soul
By Rabbi Kerry M. Olitzky 6 x 9, 160 pp, Quality PB, 978-1-879045-32-3 **$13.95**

Renewed Each Day: Daily Twelve Step Recovery Meditations Based on the Bible
By Rabbi Kerry M. Olitzky and Aaron Z.
Vol. 1—Genesis & Exodus: 6 x 9, 224 pp, Quality PB, 978-1-879045-12-5 **$14.95**
Vol. 2—Leviticus, Numbers & Deuteronomy: 6 x 9, 280 pp, Quality PB, 978-1-879045-13-2 **$18.99**

Twelve Jewish Steps to Recovery: A Personal Guide to Turning from Alcoholism & Other Addictions—Drugs, Food, Gambling, Sex ...
By Rabbi Kerry M. Olitzky and Stuart A. Copans, MD; Preface by Abraham J. Twerski, MD
6 x 9, 144 pp, Quality PB, 978-1-879045-09-5 **$14.95**

Life Cycle
Marriage / Parenting / Family / Aging

Jewish Fathers: A Legacy of Love
Photographs by Lloyd Wolf. Essays by Paula Wolfson. Foreword by Rabbi Harold Kushner.
Honors the role of contemporary Jewish fathers in America. Each father tells in his own words what it means to be a parent and Jewish, and what he learned from his own father. Insightful photos.
10¾ x 9⅞, 144 pp with 100+ duotone photos, HC, 978-1-58023-204-3 **$30.00**

The New Jewish Baby Album: Creating and Celebrating the Beginning of a Spiritual Life—A Jewish Lights Companion
By the Editors at Jewish Lights. Foreword by Anita Diamant. Preface by Rabbi Sandy Eisenberg Sasso.
A spiritual keepsake that will be treasured for generations. More than just a memory book, *shows you how—and why it's important*—to create a Jewish home and a Jewish life. 8 x 10, 64 pp, Deluxe Padded HC, Full-color illus., 978-1-58023-138-1 **$19.95**

The Jewish Pregnancy Book: A Resource for the Soul, Body & Mind during Pregnancy, Birth & the First Three Months
By Sandy Falk, MD, and Rabbi Daniel Judson, with Steven A. Rapp
Includes medical information, prayers and rituals for each stage of pregnancy, from a liberal Jewish perspective. 7 x 10, 208 pp, Quality PB, b/w photos, 978-1-58023-178-7 **$16.95**

Celebrating Your New Jewish Daughter: Creating Jewish Ways to Welcome Baby Girls into the Covenant—New and Traditional Ceremonies By Debra Nussbaum Cohen;
Foreword by Rabbi Sandy Eisenberg Sasso 6 x 9, 272 pp, Quality PB, 978-1-58023-090-2 **$18.95**

The New Jewish Baby Book, 2nd Edition: Names, Ceremonies & Customs—A Guide for
Today's Families *By Anita Diamant* 6 x 9, 336 pp, Quality PB, 978-1-58023-251-7 **$19.99**

Parenting As a Spiritual Journey: Deepening Ordinary and Extraordinary Events into
Sacred Occasions *By Rabbi Nancy Fuchs-Kreimer*
6 x 9, 224 pp, Quality PB, 978-1-58023-016-2 **$16.95**

Parenting Jewish Teens: A Guide for the Perplexed
By Joanne Doades 6 x 9, 200 pp, Quality PB, 978-1-58023-305-7 **$16.99**

Judaism for Two: A Spiritual Guide for Strengthening and Celebrating Your
Loving Relationship *By Rabbi Nancy Fuchs-Kreimer and Rabbi Nancy H. Wiener; Foreword by Rabbi Elliot N. Dorff* Addresses the ways Jewish teachings can enhance and strengthen committed relationships. 6 x 9, 224 pp, Quality PB, 978-1-58023-254-8 **$16.99**

Embracing the Covenant: Converts to Judaism Talk About Why & How
By Rabbi Allan Berkowitz and Patti Moskovitz 6 x 9, 192 pp, Quality PB, 978-1-879045-50-7 **$16.95**

The Guide to Jewish Interfaith Family Life: An InterfaithFamily.com Handbook
Edited by Ronnie Friedland and Edmund Case 6 x 9, 384 pp, Quality PB, 978-1-58023-153-4 **$18.95**

Introducing My Faith and My Community
The Jewish Outreach Institute Guide for the Christian in a Jewish Interfaith Relationship
By Rabbi Kerry M. Olitzky 6 x 9, 176 pp, Quality PB, 978-1-58023-192-3 **$16.99**

Making a Successful Jewish Interfaith Marriage: The Jewish Outreach Institute Guide
to Opportunities, Challenges and Resources *By Rabbi Kerry M. Olitzky with Joan Peterson Littman*
6 x 9, 176 pp, Quality PB, 978-1-58023-170-1 **$16.95**

The Creative Jewish Wedding Book: A Hands-On Guide to New & Old
Traditions, Ceremonies & Celebrations *By Gabrielle Kaplan-Mayer*
9 x 9, 288 pp, b/w photos, Quality PB, 978-1-58023-194-7 **$19.99**

Divorce Is a Mitzvah: A Practical Guide to Finding Wholeness and Holiness
When Your Marriage Dies *By Rabbi Perry Netter; Afterword by Rabbi Laura Geller.*
6 x 9, 224 pp, Quality PB, 978-1-58023-172-5 **$16.95**

A Heart of Wisdom: Making the Jewish Journey from Midlife through the Elder Years
Edited by Susan Berrin; Foreword by Harold Kushner
6 x 9, 384 pp, Quality PB, 978-1-58023-051-3 **$18.95**

So That Your Values Live On: Ethical Wills and How to Prepare Them
Edited by Jack Riemer and Nathaniel Stampfer
6 x 9, 272 pp, Quality PB, 978-1-879045-34-7 **$18.99**

Holidays/Holy Days

Rosh Hashanah Readings: Inspiration, Information and Contemplation
Yom Kippur Readings: Inspiration, Information and Contemplation
Edited by Rabbi Dov Peretz Elkins with Section Introductions from Arthur Green's These Are the Words
An extraordinary collection of readings, prayers and insights that enable the modern worshiper to enter into the spirit of the High Holy Days in a personal and powerful way, permitting the meaning of the Jewish New Year to enter the heart.
RHR: 6 x 9, 400 pp, HC, 978-1-58023-239-5 **$24.99**
YKR: 6 x 9, 368 pp, HC, 978-1-58023-271-5 **$24.99**

Jewish Holidays: A Brief Introduction for Christians
By Rabbi Kerry M. Olitzky and Rabbi Daniel Judson
5½ x 8½, 176 pp, Quality PB, 978-1-58023-302-6 **$16.99**

Leading the Passover Journey: The Seder's Meaning Revealed, the Haggadah's Story Retold *By Rabbi Nathan Laufer*
Uncovers the hidden meaning of the Seder's rituals and customs.
6 x 9, 224 pp, HC, 978-1-58023-211-1 **$24.99**

Reclaiming Judaism as a Spiritual Practice: Holy Days and Shabbat
By Rabbi Goldie Milgram
7 x 9, 272 pp, Quality PB, 978-1-58023-205-0 **$19.99**

7th Heaven: Celebrating Shabbat with Rebbe Nachman of Breslov
By Moshe Mykoff with the Breslov Research Institute
5⅛ x 8¼, 224 pp, Deluxe PB w/flaps, 978-1-58023-175-6 **$18.95**

The Women's Passover Companion: Women's Reflections on the Festival of Freedom *Edited by Rabbi Sharon Cohen Anisfeld, Tara Mohr, and Catherine Spector*
Groundbreaking. A provocative conversation about women's relationships to Passover as well as the roots and meanings of women's seders.
6 x 9, 352 pp, Quality PB, 978-1-58023-231-9 **$19.99**

The Women's Seder Sourcebook: Rituals & Readings for Use at the Passover Seder *Edited by Rabbi Sharon Cohen Anisfeld, Tara Mohr, and Catherine Spector*
Gathers the voices of more than one hundred women in readings, personal and creative reflections, commentaries, blessings, and ritual suggestions that can be incorporated into your Passover celebration.
6 x 9, 384 pp, Quality PB, 978-1-58023-232-6 **$19.99**

Creating Lively Passover Seders: A Sourcebook of Engaging Tales, Texts & Activities
By David Arnow, PhD 7 x 9, 416 pp, Quality PB, 978-1-58023-184-8 **$24.99**

Hanukkah, 2nd Edition: The Family Guide to Spiritual Celebration
By Dr. Ron Wolfson. Edited by Joel Lurie Grishaver.
7 x 9, 240 pp, illus., Quality PB, 978-1-58023-122-0 **$18.95**

The Jewish Family Fun Book: Holiday Projects, Everyday Activities, and Travel Ideas
with Jewish Themes *By Danielle Dardashti and Roni Sarig. Illus. by Avi Katz.*
6 x 9, 288 pp, 70+ b/w illus. & diagrams, Quality PB, 978-1-58023-171-8 **$18.95**

The Jewish Gardening Cookbook: Growing Plants & Cooking for Holidays
& Festivals *By Michael Brown* 6 x 9, 224 pp, 30+ b/w illus., Quality PB, 978-1-58023-116-9 **$16.95**

The Jewish Lights Book of Fun Classroom Activities: Simple and Seasonal
Projects for Teachers and Students *By Danielle Dardashti and Roni Sarig*
6 x 9, 240 pp, Quality PB, 978-1-58023-206-7 **$19.99**

Passover, 2nd Edition: The Family Guide to Spiritual Celebration
By Dr. Ron Wolfson with Joel Lurie Grishaver 7 x 9, 352 pp, Quality PB, 978-1-58023-174-9 **$19.95**

Shabbat, 2nd Edition: The Family Guide to Preparing for and Celebrating the Sabbath
By Dr. Ron Wolfson 7 x 9, 320 pp, illus., Quality PB, 978-1-58023-164-0 **$19.99**

Sharing Blessings: Children's Stories for Exploring the Spirit of the Jewish Holidays
By Rahel Musleah and Rabbi Michael Klayman
8½ x 11, 64 pp, Full-color illus., HC, 978-1-879045-71-2 **$18.95** *For ages 6 & up*

Children's Books
by Sandy Eisenberg Sasso

Adam & Eve's First Sunset: God's New Day
Engaging new story explores fear and hope, faith and gratitude in ways that will delight kids and adults—inspiring us to bless each of God's days and nights.
9 x 12, 32 pp, Full-color illus., HC, 978-1-58023-177-0 **$17.95** *For ages 4 & up*

Also Available as a Board Book: **Adam and Eve's New Day**
5 x 5, 24 pp, Full-color illus., Board, 978-1-59473-205-8 **$7.99** *For ages 0–4 (A SkyLight Paths book)*

But God Remembered
Stories of Women from Creation to the Promised Land
Four different stories of women—Lillith, Serach, Bityah, and the Daughters of Z—teach us important values through their faith and actions.
9 x 12, 32 pp, Full-color illus., HC, 978-1-879045-43-9 **$16.95** *For ages 8 & up*

Cain & Abel: Finding the Fruits of Peace
Shows children that we have the power to deal with anger in positive ways. Provides questions for kids and adults to explore together.
9 x 12, 32 pp, Full-color illus., HC, 978-1-58023-123-7 **$16.95** *For ages 5 & up*

God in Between
If you wanted to find God, where would you look? This magical, mythical tale teaches that God can be found where we are: within all of us and the relationships between us.
9 x 12, 32 pp, Full-color illus., HC, 978-1-879045-86-6 **$16.95** *For ages 4 & up*

God's Paintbrush: Special 10th Anniversary Edition
Wonderfully interactive, invites children of all faiths and backgrounds to encounter God through moments in their own lives. Provides questions adult and child can explore together.
11 x 8½, 32 pp, Full-color illus., HC, 978-1-58023-195-4 **$17.95** *For ages 4 & up*

Also Available: **God's Paintbrush Teacher's Guide**
8½ x 11, 32 pp, PB, 978-1-879045-57-6 **$8.95**

God's Paintbrush Celebration Kit
A Spiritual Activity Kit for Teachers and Students of All Faiths, All Backgrounds
Additional activity sheets available:
8-Student Activity Sheet Pack (40 sheets/5 sessions), 978-1-58023-058-2 **$19.95**
Single-Student Activity Sheet Pack (5 sessions), 978-1-58023-059-9 **$3.95**

In God's Name
Like an ancient myth in its poetic text and vibrant illustrations, this award-winning modern fable about the search for God's name celebrates the diversity and, at the same time, the unity of all people.
9 x 12, 32 pp, Full-color illus., HC, 978-1-879045-26-2 **$16.99** *For ages 4 & up*

Also Available as a Board Book: **What Is God's Name?**
5 x 5, 24 pp, Board, Full-color illus., 978-1-893361-10-2 **$7.99** *For ages 0–4 (A SkyLight Paths book)*

Also Available: **In God's Name video and study guide**
Computer animation, original music, and children's voices. 18 min. **$29.99**

Also Available in Spanish: **El nombre de Dios**
9 x 12, 32 pp, Full-color illus., HC, 978-1-893361-63-8 **$16.95** *(A SkyLight Paths book)*

Noah's Wife: The Story of Naamah
When God tells Noah to bring the animals of the world onto the ark, God also calls on Naamah, Noah's wife, to save each plant on Earth. Based on an ancient text.
9 x 12, 32 pp, Full-color illus., HC, 978-1-58023-134-3 **$16.95** *For ages 4 & up*

Also Available as a Board Book: **Naamah, Noah's Wife**
5 x 5, 24 pp, Full-color illus., Board, 978-1-893361-56-0 **$7.95** *For ages 0–4 (A SkyLight Paths book)*

For Heaven's Sake: Finding God in Unexpected Places
9 x 12, 32 pp, Full-color illus., HC, 978-1-58023-054-4 **$16.95** *For ages 4 & up*

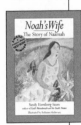

God Said Amen: Finding the Answers to Our Prayers
9 x 12, 32 pp, Full-color illus., HC, 978-1-58023-080-3 **$16.95** *For ages 4 & up*

Congregation Resources

The Art of Public Prayer, 2nd Edition: Not for Clergy Only By Lawrence A. Hoffman
6 x 9, 272 pp, Quality PB, 978-1-893361-06-5 **$19.99** *(A SkyLight Paths book)*

Becoming a Congregation of Learners: Learning as a Key to Revitalizing
Congregational Life By Isa Aron, PhD; Foreword by Rabbi Lawrence A. Hoffman
6 x 9, 304 pp, Quality PB, 978-1-58023-089-6 **$19.95**

Finding a Spiritual Home: How a New Generation of Jews Can Transform the
American Synagogue By Rabbi Sidney Schwarz
6 x 9, 352 pp, Quality PB, 978-1-58023-185-5 **$19.95**

Jewish Pastoral Care, 2nd Edition: A Practical Handbook from Traditional &
Contemporary Sources Edited by Rabbi Dayle A. Friedman
6 x 9, 528 pp, HC, 978-1-58023-221-0 **$40.00**

Jewish Spiritual Direction: An Innovative Guide from Traditional and Contemporary
Sources Edited by Rabbi Howard A. Addison and Barbara Eve Breitman
6 x 9, 368 pp, HC, 978-1-58023-230-2 **$30.00**

The Self-Renewing Congregation: Organizational Strategies for Revitalizing
Congregational Life By Isa Aron, PhD; Foreword by Dr. Ron Wolfson
6 x 9, 304 pp, Quality PB, 978-1-58023-166-4 **$19.95**

Spiritual Community: The Power to Restore Hope, Commitment and Joy
By Rabbi David A. Teutsch, PhD 5½ x 8½, 144 pp, HC, 978-1-58023-270-8 **$19.99**

The Spirituality of Welcoming: How to Transform Your Congregation into a
Sacred Community By Dr. Ron Wolfson 6 x 9, 224 pp, Quality PB, 978-1-58023-244-9 **$19.99**

Rethinking Synagogues: A New Vocabulary for Congregational Life
By Rabbi Lawrence A. Hoffman 6 x 9, 240 pp, Quality PB, 978-1-58023-248-7 **$19.99**

Children's Books

What You Will See Inside a Synagogue
By Rabbi Lawrence A. Hoffman and Dr. Ron Wolfson; Full-color photos by Bill Aron
A colorful, fun-to-read introduction that explains the ways and whys of Jewish
worship and religious life.
8½ x 10½, 32 pp, Full-color photos, HC, 978-1-59473-012-2 **$17.99** *For ages 6 & up (A SkyLight Paths book)*

The Kids' Fun Book of Jewish Time
By Emily Sper 9 x 7½, 24 pp, Full-color illus., HC, 978-1-58023-311-8 **$16.99**

In God's Hands
By Lawrence Kushner and Gary Schmidt 9 x 12, 32 pp, HC, 978-1-58023-224-1 **$16.99**

Because Nothing Looks Like God
By Lawrence and Karen Kushner
Introduces children to the possibilities of spiritual life.
11 x 8½, 32 pp, Full-color illus., HC, 978-1-58023-092-6 **$16.95** *For ages 4 & up*

Also Available: **Because Nothing Looks Like God Teacher's Guide**
8½ x 11, 22 pp, PB, 978-1-58023-140-4 **$6.95** *For ages 5–8*
  Board Book Companions to *Because Nothing Looks Like God*
5 x 5, 24 pp, Full-color illus., SkyLight Paths Board Books *For ages 0–4*

What Does God Look Like? 978-1-893361-23-2 **$7.99**

How Does God Make Things Happen? 978-1-893361-24-9 **$7.95**

Where Is God? 978-1-893361-17-1 **$7.99**

The Book of Miracles: A Young Person's Guide to Jewish Spiritual Awareness
By Lawrence Kushner. All-new illustrations by the author
6 x 9, 96 pp, 2-color illus., HC, 978-1-879045-78-1 **$16.95** *For ages 9 and up*

In Our Image: God's First Creatures
By Nancy Sohn Swartz 9 x 12, 32 pp, Full-color illus., HC, 978-1-879045-99-6 **$16.95** *For ages 4 & up*

Also Available as a Board Book: **How Did the Animals Help God?**
5 x 5, 24 pp, Board, Full-color illus., 978-1-59473-044-3 **$7.99** *For ages 0–4 (A SkyLight Paths book)*

Bar/Bat Mitzvah

The JGirl's Guide: The Young Jewish Woman's Handbook for Coming of Age
By Penina Adelman, Ali Feldman, and Shulamit Reinharz
An inspirational, interactive guidebook designed to help pre-teen Jewish girls address the spiritual, educational, and psychological issues surrounding coming of age in today's society. 6 x 9, 240 pp, Quality PB, 978-1-58023-215-9 **$14.99**

 Also Available: **The JGirl's Teacher's and Parent's Guide**
8½ x 11, 56 pp, PB, 978-1-58023-225-8 **$8.99**

Bar/Bat Mitzvah Basics: A Practical Family Guide to Coming of Age Together
Edited by Cantor Helen Leneman 6 x 9, 240 pp, Quality PB, 978-1-58023-151-0 **$18.95**

The Bar/Bat Mitzvah Memory Book, 2nd Edition: An Album for Treasuring the Spiritual Celebration *By Rabbi Jeffrey K. Salkin and Nina Salkin*
8 x 10, 48 pp, Deluxe HC, 2-color text, ribbon marker, 978-1-58023-263-0 **$19.99**

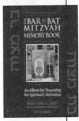

For Kids—Putting God on Your Guest List: How to Claim the Spiritual Meaning of Your Bar or Bat Mitzvah *By Rabbi Jeffrey K. Salkin*
6 x 9, 144 pp, Quality PB, 978-1-58023-015-5 **$14.99** *For ages 11–13*

Putting God on the Guest List, 3rd Edition: How to Reclaim the Spiritual Meaning of Your Child's Bar or Bat Mitzvah *By Rabbi Jeffrey K. Salkin*
6 x 9, 224 pp, Quality PB, 978-1-58023-222-7 **$16.99**; HC, 978-1-58023-260-9 **$24.99**

 Also Available: **Putting God on the Guest List Teacher's Guide**
8½ x 11, 48 pp, PB, 978-1-58023-226-5 **$8.99**

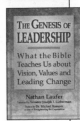

Tough Questions Jews Ask: A Young Adult's Guide to Building a Jewish Life
By Rabbi Edward Feinstein 6 x 9, 160 pp, Quality PB, 978-1-58023-139-8 **$14.99** *For ages 12 & up*

 Also Available: **Tough Questions Jews Ask Teacher's Guide**
8½ x 11, 72 pp, PB, 978-1-58023-187-9 **$8.95**

Bible Study/Midrash

Abraham's Bind & Other Bible Tales of Trickery, Folly, Mercy and Love *By Michael J. Caduto*
Re-imagines many biblical characters, retelling their stories and highlighting their foibles and strengths, their struggles and joys. Readers will learn that God has a way of working for them and through them, even today.
6 x 9, 224 pp, PB, 978-1-59473-186-0 **$19.99** *(A SkyLight Paths book)*

Ancient Secrets: Using the Stories of the Bible to Improve Our Everyday Lives
By Rabbi Levi Meier, PhD 5½ x 8½, 288 pp, Quality PB, 978-1-58023-064-3 **$16.95**

The Genesis of Leadership: What the Bible Teaches Us about Vision, Values and Leading Change *By Rabbi Nathan Laufer; Foreword by Senator Joseph I. Lieberman*
Unlike other books on leadership, this one is rooted in the stories of the Bible, and teaches the values that the Bible believes are prerequisites for true leadership.
6 x 9, 288 pp, HC, 978-1-58023-241-8 **$24.99**

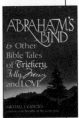

Hineini in Our Lives: Learning How to Respond to Others through 14 Biblical Texts and Personal Stories *By Norman J. Cohen* 6 x 9, 240 pp, Quality PB, 978-1-58023-274-6 **$16.99**

Moses and the Journey to Leadership: Timeless Lessons of Effective Management from the Bible and Today's Leaders *By Dr. Norman J. Cohen* 6 x 9, 240 pp, HC, 978-1-58023-227-2 **$21.99**

Self, Struggle & Change: Family Conflict Stories in Genesis and Their Healing Insights for Our Lives *By Norman J. Cohen* 6 x 9, 224 pp, Quality PB, 978-1-879045-66-8 **$18.99**

The Triumph of Eve & Other Subversive Bible Tales *By Matt Biers-Ariel*
5½ x 8½, 192 pp, HC, 978-1-59473-040-5 **$19.99** *(A SkyLight Paths book)*

Voices from Genesis: Guiding Us through the Stages of Life *By Norman J. Cohen*
6 x 9, 192 pp, Quality PB, 978-1-58023-118-3 **$16.95**

JEWISH LIGHTS BOOKS ARE AVAILABLE FROM BETTER BOOKSTORES. TRY YOUR BOOKSTORE FIRST.

About Jewish Lights

People of all faiths and backgrounds yearn for books that attract, engage, educate, and spiritually inspire.

Our principal goal is to stimulate thought and help all people learn about who the Jewish People are, where they come from, and what the future can be made to hold. While people of our diverse Jewish heritage are the primary audience, our books speak to people in the Christian world as well and will broaden their understanding of Judaism and the roots of their own faith.

We bring to you authors who are at the forefront of spiritual thought and experience. While each has something different to say, they all say it in a voice that you can hear.

Our books are designed to welcome you and then to engage, stimulate, and inspire. We judge our success not only by whether or not our books are beautiful and commercially successful, but by whether or not they make a difference in your life.

For your information and convenience, at the back of this book we have provided a list of other Jewish Lights books you might find interesting and useful. They cover all the categories of your life:

Stuart M. Matlins, Publisher

Or phone, fax, mail or e-mail to: **JEWISH LIGHTS Publishing**
Sunset Farm Offices, Route 4 • P.O. Box 237 • Woodstock, Vermont 05091
Tel: (802) 457-4000 • Fax: (802) 457-4004 • www.jewishlights.com
Credit card orders: (800) 962-4544 (8:30AM–5:30PM ET Monday–Friday)
Generous discounts on quantity orders. SATISFACTION GUARANTEED. Prices subject to change.

For more information about each book, visit our website at www.jewishlights.com